To the Rescue
Tales from the Gentle Giants Draft Horse Rescue

by Sarah J. Dufendach

TO THE RESCUE

TALES FROM THE GENTLE GIANT DRAFT HORSE RESCUE

by Sarah J. Dufendach

MINERVA RISING
PRESS

Tampa

ISBN 978-1-950811-04-5

Cover Art by Jessica Hunter-Hinsvark
Book design by Brooke Schultz

Printed and bound in USA
First Printing April 2020

Published by Minerva Rising Press
9501 Bessie Coleman Blvd #21802
Tampa, FL 33622-1082

www.minervarising.com

To my Husband, Alan Kadrofske
My toughest editor and my best supporter
Whose laugh is my favorite sound in the world

Welcome to the Gentle Giants Draft Horse Rescue

Contents

FOREWARD

I recall the first day I met Sarah Dufendach. It was a crowded Volunteer Orientation day at Gentle Giants, and I didn't really want to be there. A last-minute cancellation pulled me from my regular duties to instead meet a fresh group of potential new volunteers. Many people come to us as potential volunteers, only to drift away once the reality of real, hard work becomes clear to them. This group contained mostly young faces, seasoned riders and people who had farming written into their skin. Even so, the likelihood of seeing them return to the rescue was low. The riders would realize that volunteering is more time on a pitchfork than in a saddle, and the farm kids would tire of doing the same thing they do at home but simply someplace else. And smack in the middle of this group stood Sarah, older by two decades, trembling with nervous anticipation, and wearing boots that clearly betrayed her lack of knowledge around a barnyard. She grinned goofily, from ear to ear. She had highlights, polished nails, eyeliner and curled hair. I didn't know what to make of this woman. Was she lost? Was she listening to how hard I was telling her this would be? Did she think I was kidding?

Despite my prediction and to my surprise, Sarah came back. With eternally beaming eyes and a grating optimism, Sarah jumped right in. Please understand, Sarah doesn't just wear her heart on her sleeve—she wears it pinned to her chest in neon colors for all to see. Sensitive to both people and animals and easily tearing up at the smallest hint of equine discomfort, I wondered if she was too soft for this work. I figured we would see her a few times and then she, too, would drift away.

But Sarah kept coming back, and to this day, she has never hardened. She remains soft and raw and open to both the joy and the heartache of it all, and that is her strength. She embraces all that is the world of equine rescue, with a vulnerability that borders on fierce.

As Sarah takes you along on her Gentle Giants journey, I hope her experiences open your imagination and you see the horses with the childlike wonder of her eyes. Gentle Giants is not merely a place that exists physically in the rolling hills of Maryland. It's also a dream shared and held by volunteers, donors, and supporters to create a better world for the majestic horses to whom we owe so much. It's the place in our hearts that sees every animal in a kinder light and wants to make the rough edges of the world just a little softer for that being. I hope you enter her stories and carry them with you into your own world with animals. After all, we are all here together.

Christine Hajek,
President and Founder
Gentle Giants Draft Horse Rescue
Mt. Airey, Maryland

PREFACE

Gentle Giants Draft Horse Rescue, located in Howard County, Maryland, is home to a hundred or more draft horses rescued from abuse, cruelty and dangerous situations. Its lush pastures, woods, and horse trails are also home to rescued pigs, goats, draft mules, and a few other animals who wandered in and never left.

Draft horses, larger than other horse breeds, are the powerful Belgians, Percherons, the Suffolk Punch, Clydesdales, and Shires. They once were the sturdy horses of medieval jousting and war horses. Since the early days of our country, they plowed the fields that created our family farms, many of which still use draft horses for heavy work. They pull our carriages, police our streets and haul our beer, if only in commercials. They are often six feet tall, measured from ground to shoulder and easily weigh two thousand pounds. Yes, one ton. Their size can be intimidating, but they are calm, sweet-tempered, intelligent, awe-inspiring majestic beauties.

The Rescue often works with law enforcement authorities and animal welfare organizations around the country in cruelty cases where horses must be seized from abusive owners. It also saves horses from being sold in the United States only to be transported to Canadian or Mexican slaughterhouses where they suffer a horrible death and their meat is taken for human consumption.

The horses in the Rescue's care are rehabilitated with food, shelter, medical care, love, and whatever else is required to bring them back to good health and soundness. The horses are then retrained as riding, eventing, trail, even dressage horses and, in a few cases, jumpers. When they are ready, they can be adopted by people the Rescue has rigorously vetted.

Rescue, Rehab, Retrain, and Rehome is the Rescue's motto.

Their mission couldn't be accomplished without the dedication of a faithful, skilled staff committed to doing whatever it takes to rehabilitate the horses. A cadre of farriers dealing with hoof care, veterinarians, and other horse care professionals are also ready at all times of the day or night to apply their expertise in solving problems and finding innovative ways of treating these special horses. Two hundred thirty-seven active volunteers work alongside the staff. While that seems like a big number, and it is, it reflects the tremendous joy that comes from sharing the journey of these rescued horses as they reclaim their lives.

These horses have endured all manner of abuse and cruelty. Their bodies are sometimes hard to look at and their stories hard to hear. But no matter what condition they are in, where they come from or how they got there, once at the Rescue, they are enveloped in a big warm blanket of love and tenderness. Their story becomes all about recovery, mending broken bones and broken spirits.

While the hard work and attention given to the horses at the Rescue account for most of their recovery, there is a touch of magic about the place, an alchemy where damaged, unwanted horses are turned into priceless animals with superpowers that charm and steal your heart.

INTRODUCTION

Call it coincidence, call it fate. Whatever you call it, I came to know the abused horses at the Gentle Giants Draft Horse Rescue at turning points in their lives and in mine. The horses had been rescued from hellish situations and were recovering. Their abuse was behind them. I was ending a non-stop forty-year career as a hard-charging workaholic and was searching for something to help me cope with one of the hardest transitions of my life.

The more time I spent with the horses at the Rescue, the more I did not want to forget remarkable things, large and small, that were happening all around me. Usually when I had an observation I wanted to remember, I wrote it down on a napkin or a scrap of paper that, jammed into my pocket, turned up a shredded mess in the washing machine. This time was different.

This time, I bought a small, cardboard spiral notebook at a funky used bookshop in Washington, D.C. It was made of "100% post-consumer-waste recycled pages." The name printed on it was the "Decomposition Book." I liked it that the notebook where I would write about transition and change was itself a product of transition and change. I took it everywhere. It was small enough to put in my purse or slip into my pocket but big enough to escape the laundry.

Since I started volunteering at the Rescue four years ago, I have had three major joint replacements—two hips and a knee. While recuperating from the first of these surgeries, I began organizing the random notes I had written in my Decomposition Book. I did it for myself so I would remember the details of incidents I had enjoyed. As I rewrote my notes, the stories emerged. While recuperating from the next surgery six months later, the book came together. I finished it while recovering from a total knee replacement four years after I wrote, *My First Giant*. It's funny, to recognize now, that my decomposing joints facilitated the composition of this book.

I hope these stories entertain readers unfamiliar with horses as well as aficionados. The stories are drawn from my personal experiences and, while I have tried very hard to get the technical details of horsemanship right, any inaccuracies are mine and mine alone. I ask readers who know more about horses than I do to go easy on me.

For the most part, I see life through a humorous lens. People are funny. Animals are funny. And while I experienced intense sorrow and anger while at the Rescue, the overriding atmosphere is one of joy, fun, compassion and good humor. So I hope you readers enjoy a chuckle or two as you make your way through the book.

I have an abiding respect and love for the Rescue staff and the volunteers who make the Rescue a place like no other. From the vantage point of working alongside them, I watched them spin magic—every day. They put the animals before themselves—every day. They worried over them, tried this way if that way didn't work, until they produced the miraculous results that left me in awe. This book is a big fat kiss to them all.

Now, I invite you to come with me on an adventure to meet these inspiring horses and people on a unique journey to the Rescue.

Rescued horses came in all shapes, sizes and age. Apollo, left, and Artemis, right.

FINDING THE RESCUE
Following the Dream

My adventures at the Rescue were a result, as so many good things are, of discontent and a need for change. I wasn't seeking the Gentle Giants Draft Horse Rescue. I didn't even know it existed. But I had been making space in my life for something new, sending cosmic feelers out for something to help deal with a growing impatience that was making me increasingly edgy. I was looking for more. Little did I know I was creating the conditions for finding the Rescue.

For almost four decades, I thrived on the responsibility, fast pace, and adrenalin rush I got from my high-powered, top level jobs. I was Chief of Staff for a Member of the United States Congress, Chief Operating Officer for a multi-million dollar international non-profit, Vice President for a good-government watchdog organization, and Vice President at a large public university. Though I had a great deal of independence in all my jobs, I had learned to adapt myself to good and bad organizational structures, to bosses with a variety of personal styles (some easy, some not), and to Boards of Directors (some good, many clueless).

But now, I was chafing at those external restraints. I was restless. I felt like I was in a straitjacket. I was done adapting to outside forces over which I had little control but that had control over me. I wanted to decide what I would do and how I would do it. I wanted to be the judge of the value and quality of my work. I needed to be on my own in order to come into my own. I needed space and time to see what I would dream up for myself. That was never going to happen working the hours I did and given the responsibilities I had. If I was serious, I needed to leave the professional world of work.

Change is hard. Even when you bring it on yourself, transitioning is tough. Thinking about leaving what I knew well for something that didn't yet exist was scary. To figure out what was next, I didn't need a boss, but I did need a plan. Even if I never followed it, I needed an idea of what I wanted to do in my new world. I had developed many strategic plans throughout my career. That process focused my mind on big goals and how to achieve them. Maybe that same process could work for me now. I started making a strategic plan for my retirement.

First, I stopped calling it "retirement" and started calling it "repurposing." Retirement was never my word. It made me break out into hives. The idea of being "used up" and getting closer to the end game freaked me out. I did not want my new adventure to be described by a word containing "tired" in it. I was not tired. I did not want to withdraw; I wanted to embrace. I looked at what I was doing more like a quest. Repurposing focused on what was coming rather than on what had been.

The second thing was to identify my goals. My first stab at it looked like every discarded New Year's resolution list I had ever made: lose weight, exercise more, eat better, be nicer, blah blah blah. Those were not goals. They were tedious, worn out scoldings. My new repurposing could not start with old self-admonishments. I decided the real goal was, put simply, to be happy.

I started making a list of what I wanted more of in my life that made me happy. I already knew what I wanted less of. First, I listed spending more quality time with my husband, Alan, and our beloved Keeshond dog, Harry. Next came having more fun time with friends and family. But then a strange thing happened. I wrote the word "horses."

This came out of the blue. I hadn't come near a horse in nearly fifty years. Horses had taken up exactly zero of my day-to-day brain space. But there it was, nearing the top of my list. Puzzled, I just stared at the word hoping what was behind it would come to me. It did. As a little girl growing up in Detroit, Michigan, in the 1950s, I had been completely obsessed with all things equine.

Back then, Detroit was known as the "Motor City." The car was king and gearheads ruled. Muscle cars were all the rage and horsepower was everything. But the only horsepower I truly cared anything about was Roy Roger's magnificent palomino, Trigger, the Lone Ranger's trusty horse, Silver, and the other horses I saw on TV or read about in books. I played with plastic horse action figures like other little girls played with Barbie dolls. I pretended the tired old trail horses at the stable where I got to ride once a year on the family vacation were Misty of Chincoteague, Black Beauty, Flicka, or the Black Stallion pounding down the back stretch.

As I got older, I became a city girl with city ways. I used public transportation and carried stuff in a New York Times tote bag. I "did lunch" and the theatre after work. I owned fifteen black skirts, six black leather briefcases of varying size and a staggering number of black high heel shoes.

Apparently, the spell cast over me long ago still had energy. Time had not completely worn away my youthful enchantment. By putting horses on my list, I had clearly made a wish. And a wish, sincerely made, is a powerful thing. I started getting solicitations in the mail from horse rescues. I had never gotten solicitations like that before. Suddenly, there were calendars from Colorado, pictures from Arizona, and postcards from horse rescues in California and all over the country. I figured this was an opportunity to engage with horses even if I could not see or touch them. I picked an envelope out of the pile at random and sent a check.

A couple of months later I got a note from the Gentle Giants Draft Horse Rescue in Maryland, thanking me for my contribution. They invited me to their facility to see how my money was being used. Only then did I notice I had picked a rescue that was only about 1.5 hours from our house in Northern Virginia.

I made an appointment and Alan and I went to the Rescue. Alan did not share my love of horses. He had been on a horse once a long time ago at a public riding stable in Michigan. The horse he was on slowly meandered a little way beyond the barn, turned around and trotted back to its stall. He remembers bouncing around on that horse like a rag doll while hanging on for dear life. Alan is over six feet tall. He had to practically fold himself in half, ducking in the saddle to avoid slamming his head on the low cross beam of the barn door as his horse ran back in. Not tempted himself by what a horse rescue might offer, he knew how much I wanted to go and was happy to come with me, as long as he didn't have to ride anything.

We didn't know what to expect as we left Northern Virginia and the city of Washington, D.C. behind us heading north into rural Maryland. It was early April. The air got cooler and the ground got muddier the farther north we went. As we came closer to the Rescue, the directions we were given over the phone became vague. They were less about precise crossroads, street names, and route numbers and more about descriptions of bendy curves in the road and turning at mailbox clusters with blue recycling cans.

My heart started pounding when we turned onto the Rescue's gravel driveway and I spotted the first field of horses. I had only seen Belgians in picture books. I already thought they were beautiful. To my great delight, there were three in that first field. The contrast between their blonde mane and tails and the coppery color of their bodies was breathtaking. One was running, the wind in its mane, showing off the color combo to maximum effect. There were white horses, chestnut colored horses, blacks, and a paint. I leaned way out of the car window to see better. I got the first whiff of the horses. It was sweet and earthy, like a rare exotic perfume.

As we got closer to the field, the horses became as curious about us as I was about them. The driveway went up to a metal gate. A few horses and a mule crowded around it. Some stretched their necks to get a good look at us. Others nipped and jostled each other, vying for the prime spot where the gate might open to let them out or where people with food might come in. I was almost close enough to touch them. They were more beautiful than I could have ever imagined. One black Percheron, especially tall and powerful, looked like a horse the mythical Norse Valkyries would have ridden down from Valhalla. It didn't take much imagination for me to see giant wings on his back and fire shooting from his nostrils.

Continuing up the gravel driveway, I could see we were coming to a vast two-story white barn with a high-pitched roof. Imposing as the barn was, it was the chickens and peacocks running around that grabbed my attention. Goats, sheep, cats, dogs, and the fattest, loudest pig I had ever seen or heard, formed our welcoming committee. I decided, before I even got out of the car, I wanted to be part of this.

Everything on this beautiful one hundred thirty six acre place was super-sized. The twelve horse stalls in the white barn were each the size of a Washington, D.C. apartment. Behind the barn was a top-notch indoor riding arena. Birds flew around high in the rafters. I am scared to death of birds, especially in confined spaces, but the arena roof was so high it was like the birds were outside. There had just been an event and bales of hay were still stacked along one side of the arena like bleachers to accommodate an audience.

The goats and sheep shared a pen along one side of the white barn. It was so filled with things to climb onto and into that it looked like an elementary school playground. The goats and sheep were not in the pen; as during most days, they were allowed to roam around the Rescue.

Beyond the white barn and up a hill was a bright red structure called the rehabilitation barn. It was equipped to handle emergencies and horses needing specialized care. The stalls there were like luxury apartments. There was plenty of room for a draft horse to lay down, five or six people to walk around, and mounting blocks, x-ray machines, and whatever other equipment might be needed. The stalls opened onto an even bigger outside fenced-in area where an injured horse could get exercise in a safe space. It was like an apartment with attached garden.

Farther up the hill past the rehabilitation barn was a beautifully maintained outdoor riding arena. There were two more barns and six or seven run-in shelters. Beyond that were several more fields reachable only by four-wheeler. I saw Rescue staff zooming along the dirt and gravel lanes so fast their ponytails streamed out behind them. I was getting even more excited. I wanted to be racing around on the four-wheeler with them.

Impressed as I was with the barns, the arenas, and the lush fields stretching to the horizon, the horses were the stars of the Rescue. I was not prepared for their size. These horses weighed a ton. No exaggeration. They could weigh two thousand pounds when they were healthy. As we walked along the road, horses of all kinds hung their huge heads over the fences to say hello. I scratched their foreheads. Some backed away, but most were curious. They gently searched my outstretched hand looking for treats. I was in heaven.

A Belgian mare in one field had been at the Rescue for about a month. She was still painfully skinny. She trotted along the fence line with us. Her name was Skittles. She had been rescued right before she was sold at auction to a vendor for a slaughterhouse, priced by the pound, for her meat. Skittles's meat would have been exported overseas for human consumption.

The Rescue had a volunteer program where, working right along with the staff, you could feed the horses, groom them, and muck out stalls. Volunteers helped when the farriers (mobile blacksmiths) came once a week to care for the horses' hooves. Volunteers could also help the veterinarian when she came out once or twice a week. If the staff came to trust and rely on you, there was even more you could do.

The Rescue had a Sponsorship Program where people financially supporting a horse could spend individual time with them. Then there was the Rescue's Partner Program where you picked one special horse you loved to work with. Staff taught basic moves like correctly leading your horse, backing up, and getting your horse to stand still at a mounting block. They also taught how to walk and trot your horse in a circle on a long lead rope as well as special reward-based training technique. If you worked a certain number of hours each month, you might be allowed to ride the horses.

Here it was. Here was my chance to work closely with lots of horses. This all felt right. This was my wish coming true.

Walking back to the main barn, I stepped into a hole. I watched the mud ooze over my hiking boots and envelop my feet. When I tried to get out, the mud sucked my foot back down and for a minute I couldn't move. The Rescue had captured me! While Alan helped me regain my footing, I whispered to him that he might have to sedate me to get me to leave this place.

On our way home, I bounced around in the car and chattered like a little kid. In my head I was already filling out the papers to sponsor Skittles. I was planning out how many days a week I could volunteer. I was figuring out a shorter route from home that could reduce the hour and a half trip. Alan, who knows me well, looked straight at me, laughed and said, "Sarah, I know what you are thinking. But we can't move to Maryland to be closer to Skittles."

Not long after finding the Rescue, I left the professional world of work, setting in motion a profound life transition. Even though I would face situations and tasks for which I was comically unprepared, I did become a volunteer at the Rescue and I did sponsor Skittles. I traveled along with her and horses like her on their journey—from abandonment and cruelty to love and kindness, from starvation to abundance. Giving these abused horses a second chance fed my spirit. Eventually the Rescue would become a cornerstone of my own transition.

COMING TO THE RESCUE
Finding the Sweet Spot

It was obvious to everyone at the Gentle Giant Draft Horse Rescue new volunteers' orientation that I was not a typical volunteer. I was three times older than nearly everyone at the Rescue. I lived an hour and a half away in a town in another state. I did not have horses of my own or live on a farm like most of the other volunteers. I was not plugged into the horse network. And my inner athlete had long been on hiatus. But I did not care about any of that. I was over the moon at the chance to volunteer.

Christine, the Rescue's Founder and President, was ready to begin the orientation when someone handed her a note. After reading it, she told us the staff person who was going to do the orientation with her had a family emergency and would not be joining us. Her dog was sick and she had to take him to the vet. I immediately knew a place where a dog's condition was considered a "family" emergency was the right place for me, no matter how different I appeared. I wanted very badly to make this work and was ready to do whatever it took. I wanted to be a good volunteer even though, on the surface, I was a total mismatch.

There was a standing room only crowd of about twenty potential volunteers packed into the volunteer lounge. The lounge was two couches covered with old blankets, a table with a few folding chairs, a refrigerator, and a desk, all on a cement floor. What it lacked in beauty it made up for in comfort. There were shelves full of snacks, cold Gatorade and water in the fridge, pictures of horses on the walls, a coffee machine, and a blessedly efficient air conditioner.

Wasting no time, Christine called the meeting to order and was blunt. She announced right off the bat that only four or five of us would actually make it through the training program and become volunteers. She said no one needed experience at the start but we would all have to take the hands-on Horsemanship and Safety class held in the indoor arena. We would have real horses and an experienced instructor. We would have to learn to handle ourselves around the horses in order to be a volunteer. A staff person would be assigned to work side by side with each one of us for the first three or four times. I was grateful they would pay so much attention to me, but some in the crowd grumbled that they already knew all this stuff and were insulted they had to be monitored. Christine dismissed their objections. She was not going to take any risks with the horses. They had been through enough. No volunteer who thought they were above learning was going to work out.

She told us whatever we thought we knew, we had to forget. We needed to relearn everything the "Rescue Way." At first, that sounded arrogant. But she said we all had to accept the same protocols, we all had to do the same things the same way, so the horses knew what to expect from us and we knew what to expect from each other. We had to be consistent, executing proven methods to keep us all, horses included, safe.

The more Christine spoke, the clearer it became she was a ferocious protector of the Rescue's animals. A horse may have come to the Rescue an abandoned, shabby mess, but here, that horse was precious. Our value as volunteers would be measured by how well we treated the animals. I whole-heartedly embraced this code of conduct and could not wait to get started.

One of my early days at the Rescue was an August scorcher in the hottest month of the hottest year on record ever. Across the country, people were dying from the insufferable heat. Over the years, my own tolerance of the heat had virtually disappeared; basic functioning that day was going to be a challenge.

Nevertheless, that afternoon, three young women and I headed out to feed horses in the farthest reaches of the Rescue. We loaded up the four-wheeler named Donna. Donna was comically adorned with long black eyelashes painted around her headlights and big red lips painted below. When I first saw this startling vehicle and learned her name, I couldn't help softly singing the song, "Oh Donna." I was met with blank stares. I explained "Oh Donna" was recorded by the late great Richie Valens who died in a plane crash along with the legendary Buddy Holly in 1959. Still no sign of recognition. With that one act, I had established myself as ancient.

A staffer fired up Donna. After balking at the takeoff, we began picking up speed. We ground through mud, tractor tracks, gopher holes, and ruts until we were sailing along at a shocking clip. The wind in my face felt, not like a cool breeze blowing back my hair as in the cologne ads, but like a gob of Vaseline smeared over my head. A salty mix of sweat, sunscreen and makeup began seeping into my eyes, stinging like acid.

Donna came to an abrupt stop in the middle of what looked to me like nowhere. I wondered if she was broken. Had she thrown a rod or something else important? Why would we be stopping here? Oh Lord, did we kill something on that last bump?

Unconcerned, the others jumped out and unloaded the feed buckets. I was really bewildered now. I could see the horses just beyond the tall wooden slat fence, but there was no gate. How were we going to get into the field to feed them?

Then, soaked in sweat, I froze. This was not possible. I must be having a heat-induced hallucination. It looked like everyone was climbing the fence. Not just any fence, but the Great Wall of China—high enough to contain draft horses the size of mobile homes. But that did not seem to bother anyone but me, as over they went, effortlessly carrying the big feed buckets. One over, two over, three young ladies over the fence. And then there was me.

I felt cruelly ambushed. I was not ready for this. There was no warning, no instructional YouTube video. It was like that nightmare we all have of being forced to take the final exam in a class you always skipped—the one where you don't even understand the questions, let alone know the answers. I didn't know how to climb this fence.

But I was going to have to climb the damn fence or get left behind. I was going to have to climb it or prove I was, in fact, a weak link and beyond all doubt, not Gentle Giants Draft Horse Rescue volunteer material.

I grabbed the highest rail. My polished red fingernails looked like drops of blood on the weather-beaten wood. I put one foot on the lowest slat and tried to hoist myself up, but my foot slid off. That slat wasn't going to be high enough anyway. I put my foot on the next highest slat. I tried hoisting myself up again, but my foot was now so high my knee was up near my chin. I didn't have enough leverage. Holy Crap, I must have gained so much weight and lost so much muscle tone sitting behind a desk in my "Executive Positions" that I quite literally could no longer pull my own weight. I could feel my face getting hotter even though I was already at the melting point. Grabbing the top of the fence, I hauled myself up, grunting an empty promise to never again eat at my local Weenie Beanie. My arms were barely capable of pulling up my dead weight. I was getting a touch light-headed.

It was all a little confusing, but after that big effort, I do remember I got one foot going one way and my other foot going the other way on opposite sides of the top rail. My hips, one of which was a prosthetic, felt like they were going in another direction entirely. I couldn't really move forward or backward, up or even down, as the top rail was hitting me uncomfortably in the crotch. Sweat and sunscreen began running into my eyes again, blurring my vision. It didn't matter. My glasses were so steamed up from my ever-increasing internal temperature, I could only make out shadows.

I realized, through pain and embarrassment as I hung there, I was stuck on that freaking fence as surely as if someone had tied me up there with bailing wire. This was bad.

My useless glasses were now sliding down my sweaty nose. I was hanging on for dear life. Straddling the fence, my legs were not long enough to reach a lower slat to stabilize myself or to take my weight off the skinny, gnarly top rail digging into me, hurting like hell and cutting off my blood circulation. My legs were starting to go numb. I had to do something soon while I could still move.

Leaning forward on the top rail, I started to swing one leg backward up and over the fence twisting my torso as I went. Something felt wrong. Holding on tight, I still could not find a lower slat to put my feet on. I was hanging on to the top rail, but both feet were still dangling, searching for the lower slat. My already stressed arms were getting tired. Where the hell was it? The damn slat had to be close, but I couldn't I find it. When I finally looked down, searching for the slat, I realized how high up I was. I got a scary sensation of falling. I could see myself coming off the fence right onto my titanium hip. Although my fake hip was about thirteen years old and gave me no trouble, I started imagining it popping out of its socket if I hit the ground. I was getting the tiniest bit nauseous.

And then I felt gentle, sweet, Kerry, a Rescue staffer, carefully guide my foot to the next slat. "These fences are high, and we all have trouble with them," she kindly lied. She helped me put my feet in the right place and showed me how to shift my weight as I climbed down. I was insanely grateful.

When I was safely on the ground, Kerry asked, without condescension or hint of ridicule, if I would like her to show me how to climb the fence. I loved her for that. We went literally one step at a time, kind of like learning the waltz, one two three, one two three. One, grab the fence. Two, put a foot on the bottom slat. Three, lift and put second foot on the bottom slat. Repeat on the second slat. Swing one leg over the top of the fence and plant it firmly on the second slat. Shift your weight to the other side of the fence and pivot. Swing other leg over the fence. The most important thing was, always have at least one foot on the fence at all times. That minimizes the scary dangling part from the top rail. Go down the reverse way you started up, one foot at a time, one slat at a time. And that's how I learned to climb a Gentle Giant fence.

Trudging through the field to catch up with the others, nursing the inevitable sliver under my bleeding fingernail, I began mentally measuring just how far out of my comfort zone I had wandered. In my professional world, I was at the top of my game. I was the one in control. Being the boss, I knew lots of stuff. Here at the Rescue, everything was new and unfamiliar and hard. Here, I was not at the top of my game. I was not good at anything; I controlled nothing. I was just this side of becoming another heat-related fatality. My co-workers were young and fit; I was not. They knew everything about horses; I did not. Horse care and farm chores required me to do things I had not done in decades. And yet, in the midst of this great discomfort, I felt a sense of well-being. A sense of having found a good place. There was kindness here.

I did not know it then, walking in the field that day, smarting from the indignity of having to be fetched off a fence, but at the Rescue I would find my sweet spot. Not my comfort zone, I was bored with that. But a place where, even though I was frequently wrong-footed and off-balance, I would feel things on a different level. I would not be arguing the pros and cons of public policy with Members of Congress. I would be hand-feeding warm mash to an emaciated horse doing his best to survive.

That sweltering day in August was physically miserable and emotionally challenging. It was not easy admitting I no longer had the athleticism or strength of my youth when I was a tennis player and worked as a lifeguard in the summers. But unsettling as it was, I had for some time been mentally moving away from my professional life, away from my comfort zone of successes, well-worn paths, confidence, and familiar routines. The Rescue was full of scary things, people I did not know, and animals that dwarfed the farm equipment. It held embarrassments for me, large and small. But the Rescue challenged me to embrace my life in transition, and I was hungry for the change.

Me, Jinx, Ginger the mule, Dawn and Razzle in the background. At the Rescue, I would find my sweet spot.

MY FIRST GIANT
Getting Grounded

One delightful evening after all the chores were done, the staff and a few of us volunteers were hanging out in the barn not wanting to let go of the moment. Someone suggested it was a great night for a trail ride. Everyone agreed. Saddles, blankets and bridles were hauled out and horses tacked up. They asked me if I wanted to ride in the indoor arena with some of the other new volunteers. I knew there was the possibility for volunteers to have riding privileges if "appropriate," meaning if they had enough experience riding a horse and put in enough hours at the Rescue. I figured this was my chance to be cleared to ride, which I was eager to do.

I had worked with trail horses at a YWCA camp in northern Michigan two summers during college. I rode a few of them although I had never had a riding lesson. But how hard could this be? It was just a matter of showing the staff I knew my way around a horse.

Christine thought about which horse would be the best for me. She settled on a huge Belgian mare. I noticed several things about this mare as soon as she was led into the arena. I could barely see over her back and her hooves were as big as dinner plates. Her name was Twinkie. While I waited for someone to find Twinkie's saddle, I noticed riders were using both the smaller English style

saddles and the bigger Western style saddles. I thought even the English saddles looked pretty big. And then I got a good look at Twinkie's saddle. It was
a western saddle and easily the size of a Lazy-Boy recliner. The saddle horn
looked like a coiled Cobra ready to strike.

It had been half a century since I last saddled a horse. That one had been
a normal size horse, not a supersized behemoth like Twinkie. I got the saddle
blanket on her without much trouble. But I staggered as I tried to lift her saddle high enough to set it onto Twinkie's enormous back. I had to put it down,
reassess, and start again. I finally did manage to get most of it up on Twinkie,
but not before the saddle blanket fell off. I had to start over a second time.
Someone soon came to help me—mostly for Twinkie's sake, I'm pretty sure.

Once her saddle and bridle were on and the stirrups were adjusted, I realized Twinkie was so tall there was no way I was going to get on her from the
ground. Even if I could lift my foot over my head, I was still not going to reach
the stirrup. I had to mount her with the help of a three-step mounting block.
Even with the block, it was all I could do to stretch my leg up far enough to put
my foot in the stirrup. Once on, it took me a minute to adjust to the altitude. I
thought my ears might pop, like in an airplane.

Never mind it felt like the air was thinner this far off the ground, I had to
focus on riding. I was told that while they sometimes use Western style saddles,
they always rein English style at the Rescue. English style? I wondered what the
hell that was. I soon learned it was a rein in each hand, thumbs on top, thread-
ed through little fingers, elbows in, wrists flexible, on and on. What happened
to good old neck reigning where, with the reigns bunched up in one hand, you
could use your free hand to scratch your nose, keep your hair from flying into
your bubble gum, or stop your pants from riding up? I was all confused.

By now, Twinkie had me pegged as an idiot and was pretty much running
on autopilot. I was doing a lot of clucking and kicking and arm flapping while
Twinkie went wherever she wanted to—not exactly the moves of an accomplished rider in control of her horse. I could feel my "appropriateness" ebbing.

When it came time to stop riding for the evening, I steered Twinkie back
toward the mounting block so I could use it to get off the same way I had
used it to get on. I was told I didn't need the mounting block. All I had to do

was swing a leg over the saddle, kick the other leg out of the stirrup, and just "slide off." What? I thought this was a joke! I was a half-mile high up here on Twinkie. People looked like ants from up here. Just slide off!?

I kicked my foot out of the right stirrup, swung my leg over Twinkie's back, leaned all the way over the saddle on my stomach, and kicked my foot out of the left stirrup. With unease, I started letting myself slide down. I thought it was taking a long time to hit the ground, even off a horse as big as a small shed. Then I noticed I was not moving at all. My feet were dangling, but I was not going down. A sudden, sharp pain made me realize, to my horror, my bra had caught on the saddle horn and I was just hanging up there on Twinkie by my Maidenform. If I couldn't go down, the only way I could see to get free was to grab the other side of the saddle and try to haul myself back up. I could not believe this was happening! Who catches their undergarments on a saddle horn?

I grabbed for the other side of the saddle and tried to hoist myself up. I started going down instead. I pulled harder on the saddle. But that just made it loosen to the point it slid down Twinkie's side. It curled underneath her with me still stuck on the damn saddle horn! Not until the last lurch of the saddle did my bra pull free. I fell backwards on my butt. Twinkie wandered off dragging her saddle underneath her. I was sprawled out in the middle of an arena full of people and horses with my tank top all askew in a bra that now hid nothing. I have rarely ever felt less "appropriate."

I had been grounded in every sense of the word. Sitting in the sand on the arena's floor, I struggled to get my clothes back in order before I became a spectacle. I had been shown in graphic style that I had to re-think how grounded I actually was in the many aspects of horsemanship when it came to the Rescue's unique-sized horses.

Not long after this incident, Twinkie was adopted into a wonderful new home and I began taking proper riding lessons. After telling this story around the Rescue a few times, I learned that this, or some embarrassing version of it, had happened to not one or two others, but to most of the women at the Rescue. In fact, one afternoon I pushed open the heavy wooden gate into the indoor riding arena to find a friend standing next to her mount. Her baggy sweater was over her head, while her arms moved around underneath. I asked if I could help. I heard muffled laughing from under the sweater. Her head popped out. She too had caught her bra on the saddle horn getting down. But she had to actually slip out of it altogether in order to dismount. She was trying to discreetly wiggle back into it.

This adventure took place in the early days when I had just started volunteering at the Rescue, before I gained perspective. About four years after this incident occurred, I was checking with Christine to make sure I was getting a few of the details right for this book. I asked her exactly how tall Twinkie was. I had guessed about 17.3 hands high, but I wanted to make sure she wasn't taller. She said Twinkie was about 15.3 hands high. I said, "No, you remember, the big Belgian mare I rode in the arena that day early on when I first started volunteering." She said of course she knew Twinkie. She was one of the smaller Belgians. That's why they named her Twinkie!

I thought I must be in an alternate universe. I was dumbfounded. I didn't know how to respond. I had no words. To me, Twinkie was gigantic. If Paul Bunyan had a horse instead of Babe his blue ox, it would have been Twinkie. I thought she was named Twinkie ironically because she was so big. Twinkie got adopted shortly after our ride together so there was no way I could do a reality check. All I have to say is that, *to me, at that time in my adventure at the Rescue, Twinkie was massive, just as I described her. My reactions and perceptions were just as I reported.* It goes to show that even a small Belgian draft horse is a really big horse!

I suspect when I first came, other things I encountered besides Twinkie might have seemed bigger to me than they seem to me now. Maybe I need to take another good look at a particular fence.

Photo by Christina Rizzutto

After the debacle on Twinkie, I took riding lessons. Chicory, seen here and adopted from the Rescue by my instructor, really is 17.3 hands high. In the end, I did ride a giant Belgian mare, it just wasn't Twinkie.

BABIES COME TO THE RESCUE
Delighting in What Others Can Not See

Little orphan Artemis was only two months old when she took the Rescue by storm. The day she arrived started out warm and sunny but by mid-afternoon, the wind had kicked up and it started to rain. The darkening sky looked threatening.

The barn stalls were filled with horses brought in from their fields, waiting for their turn with the farrier. He came to the Rescue once a week to file hooves and make custom shoes for the horses who needed them. I had never seen a mobile farrier and thought his set up was amazing. He had an anvil, a heat source, lots of different size horseshoes, and an assortment of heavy metal files, hammers, and mallets all neatly packed in the back of his customized truck. When he backed up to the open sliding barn door, he could pound out and fit custom-made horseshoes right there in the barn. This was essential because shoes for our horses were not like shoes for other horses. Our horse's shoes were the size of manhole covers.

Several of us were keeping the horses calm while the farrier worked. Suddenly, all through the barn, our cell phone alerts started going off, warning of dangerous weather. Then we heard the thunder. As it got closer, it drowned out the sound of the farrier's hammer on the anvil. The Rescue was in the middle of a barn restoration—there were no shutters on any of the windows yet. Dirt, leaves, hay, sticks, and other debris blew in through the open windows along with the slashing rain. The wind roared so loudly we could barely hear each other even when we yelled.

As the storm gained strength, staff and volunteers soaked to the bone came blowing into the barn from all over the Rescue. The howling wind set off little eddies of debris that swirled around the barn floor. The temperature suddenly dropped. I could hear the horses pacing in their stalls. Some kicked at their stall doors creating sounds rivaling the thunder. The dogs were on high alert, running up and down the length of the barn. We got news reports on our phones that several tornadoes had touched down not far from the Rescue. Then, the electricity went out. The mid-day darkness was eerie. It was so black in the barn I could see the moon in the sky outside but not my own hands in front of my face.

On normal days, the barn was a bit of a wind tunnel, but now the wind whipping through was so strong it was hard to stand up. I felt a sense of danger. When the power first went out, our intrepid farrier was unphased. He just fired up the generator in his truck that powered a flood light and kept on pounding out a metal shoe. But now, even he had to stop. I think he would have worked despite the wind, but the horses were too spooked to let him get near them. Horses are flight animals. Fleeing scary situations has worked well for thousands of years. In their heads, they should have already been out of the barn and long gone. They were not about to give anyone control of their feet.

When the storm eased up a bit, I looked out the barn door to see what was going on outside. Despite the rain still coming down, I thought I could make out a truck and trailer coming up the Rescue's long steep gravel driveway. I blinked and looked again. No one would be out in this mess. But sure enough, a truck and a medium-sized horse trailer were slowly making their way up the driveway. The driver parked his rig and fought his way through the rain to where several of us had now gathered in the barn entrance, staring at him. He didn't look crazy. His voice was level and unhurried. He said he had driven from Kentucky and had a foal to deliver. What the Hell? Had he not noticed the sky open and spit out a tornado?

A few of us followed the driver back to his trailer to help him unload the foal. The rain made a horrible clatter pounding on the roof of the trailer. Through the wind and rain, we got that tiny little foal into the barn. She was amazingly calm as she stepped into her new home that looked like a crime scene. It was now light enough for her to see she was being greeted by a pack of four dogs, the frustrated farrier, nervous horses, drenched staff and volunteers, some chickens, two chatty baby goats, and a three-legged cat named Elvis.

Her Kentucky name was Yvette. Her new Maryland name would be Artemis. She was a long-legged bay with a beautifully shaped head. She was in remarkably good shape given the scary trip all by herself. Once situated in her stall, I petted and cooed to her, stroking her forehead. She nestled in, hanging her head over my shoulder as I pressed my cheek into her neck. She was too adorable for words. I secretly wondered if she could fit in my car and come live in my backyard.

An odd noise disrupted my daydream. Two recently rescued baby goats were poking their heads through the window of Artemis' stall. The goat complex was adjacent to the barn and shared a wall and a few windows with the horse stalls. Goats are incredibly curious animals and with no shutters on the window, Luna and Roscoe were free to check out the new arrival. They stuck their heads as far through the window into her stall as they could and bleated at her. She whinnied a high-pitched screech back and stretched her long neck up the wall until their three orphan-noses touched. A beautiful relationship was forming. Those goats were so obsessed with Artemis we could not stop them trying to launch themselves through the open window down into her stall. Sadly, we had to move Artemis into a stall without a window so the crazy goats couldn't see her.

When the storm passed, we drove around the Rescue to assess the damage. Thankfully, all the animals made it through safely and there was no serious damage to any of the buildings. A few fences were broken and lots of trees were down, but nothing catastrophic. The area surrounding the Rescue was not as lucky. Just past the entrance to our driveway, a huge tree had been up-ended, exposing a root system the size of an SUV. Smaller trees were strewn everywhere, making travel on some nearby roads impossible. Power lines were down all over. I later heard subway stations as far away as Washington D.C. had flooded. Several tornadoes did touch down in our area, making it all the more remarkable that the Rescue came through it safely.

On the long drive home, I wondered why Christine named our new foal Artemis. I never heard of the name Artemis. I thought she would pick a "bad weather" name, but we already had a Storm, Thunder, Twister, etc. And the foal's calm personality did not inspire a name like Tornado even though she had arrived in a swirl. She was calm, more like an oasis. When I got home, I checked Google. According to the baby-namer website, the name Artemis is from Greek Mythology and means "Goddess of the Moon" or "Safety." It was perfect!

The New Holland Horse Auction in Pennsylvania was a few hours' drive from the Rescue. Many horses brought to be sold there were sick or badly injured. Most of the time the people responsible for these horses did not care what happened to them or how they were treated. When there was no bid high enough, they became fair game for what was referred to as the "meat men." They bought these desperate horses by the pound to sell to the slaughter-houses in Canada and Mexico where it is legal to slaughter horses for human consumption. It is not legal to kill horses in the United States for people to eat, but it is legal to sell horses in the U.S. to be transported to slaughterhouses in other countries where it is legal.

Whenever possible, people from the Rescue went to the New Holland Auction to save as many horses as they could from the gruesome slaughter-house death where they were stunned by a bolt to the head, their throats slit, and they were strung up. And that's when it all went as planned. The first bolt didn't always stun them. Imagine for yourself what happened to the terrified horse then.

Most of the horses saved from slaughter were brought back to the Rescue and tenderly cared for and rehabilitated. But sometimes horses had suffered abuse so severe, Christine bought them and had them euthanized right there at the auction. She called them mercy buys. It was more merciful to release them from the agony that had become their lives than to leave them to a miserable death in an overcrowded trailer on the long trip to slaughter. Some mercy buys were strong enough to be brought back to the calmness of the Rescue, be fed, treated kindly and given a quick, merciful, painless passing.

One day, Christine came home from the auction with an extremely lame buckskin mare she bought as a mercy case. She was not emaciated as most mercy buys were, but her lameness had gone untreated for so long she could hardly function. It was easy to see this poor girl had once been beautiful. Christine, oddly I thought, named her Dawn. Maybe she was thinking dawn was about to break for this horse, not here, but in her new world on the "other side."

Christine kept studying her. There was something about Dawn. Finally, she said she thought Dawn was pregnant. Oh my God, how could that poor, lame little thing be carrying a baby? Dawn was tested and sure enough, she was pregnant.

New plan. There would be no euthanizing. Instead, she was fed well and received medicine to treat her lameness. She was nurtured, and she recovered as best she could. One day, I don't know how, Dawn gave birth to her little stowaway. He was her mirror image. Christine named him Apollo. My heart lifted every time I saw that pair peacefully grazing together. Most of the foals at the Rescue were orphans. Apollo was one of the few raised by his own mother. He was feisty and demanding. She was patient and gentle.

Apollo was almost lost cargo. In my eyes, he was a Miracle Baby. I whispered that to him every time I hugged him and petted his impossibly cute nose. For Dawn and Apollo, Death would have to wait. Dawn had recovered and changed her stars. A new life really did "dawn" for her and her baby—not on the other side, but right here.

The year before Artemis and Apollo arrived, five foals came to the Rescue together in one big horse trailer. They had been picked up in Kentucky. Tulip, Daisy, Gunsmoke, Juniper, and Sundance were all nurse mare foals—code for throw-aways. Our five babies were incredibly rare. Until recently, most foals like them were killed soon after they were born. It has been an ugly story.

A brood mare with a good pedigree bred to a pedigreed stallion is like the goose who lays the golden egg. Her foals bring a big price. The more times she can be bred, the more golden foals she can produce. There is no time to waste letting the mare bond with or nurse her own foal; she has to be bred again as soon as possible. Her big-money golden foal is taken away from her and given to what is known as a nurse mare to feed and raise.

Nurse mares are kept perpetually pregnant so they are ready to nurse the big-money foals. What happens when the nurse mare gives birth? Where does her baby fit in? It doesn't. It is an unwanted by-product. It's like the child's game of Musical Chairs. Except in this macabre game of Musical Mares, the foal without a mother at the end loses. And losing has meant death. It's like the owners did not even see the nurse mare foals as real horses. They were the unwanted and they needed to be gotten out of the way.

Recently, though, networks of good people in the horse-breeding business and animal-welfare organizations have begun identifying locations of the nurse mare foals and are interceding, so more of them survive. For example, the Kentucky Humane Society notified Christine about these five newborn nurse mare foals. That is how Daisy, Tulip, Juniper, Gunsmoke, and Sundance came from Kentucky to the Rescue.

I happened to be at the Rescue the day the babies came. I expected them to be misshapen with open running sores, bald spots, too weak and too timid to come out of the horse trailer. After all, they were worthless by-products that no one else wanted.

What jumped off the back of the truck or dance down the trailer ramp were the most enchanting creatures I had ever seen. I was not prepared for their overwhelming cuteness. Each one was perfect from their tiny twitching noses to their short scrub brush tails. Not an oozing scab or tumor in sight, just beautiful coats of red and brown, gold and silver. And twenty perfect teeny, tiny little hooves. I was instantly smitten.

With the arrival of these five, there were now six nurse mare foals at the Rescue. Buckshot had arrived all by himself about a month before. He was three days old when he got to the Rescue. He was taken away from his mother within the first twenty-four hours of his birth. Christine drove to Kentucky and back to get him all in one day. Buckshot was in the barn waiting for the newcomers when they arrived.

Once we got the babies out of the trailer, into their stalls and settled down, we needed to get all six of them fed. They were too young to eat grain. In fact, Daisy was not much more than a week old. Instead, each foal got a nice warm bucket of milk. The new foals took up all the extra stalls, so Buckshot got fed in the wide aisle running down the middle of the barn. He was nervous. For most of his short life, he had been the only adorable youngster at the Rescue. He regarded the new babies as dangerous invaders. He was grumpy. He was jealous. He was looking to disrupt.

I was so fascinated with the new babies that I never saw it coming. Buckshot had maneuvered his rear end close to his milk bucket. He gave it a fast, hard kick, sending it soaring. It sounded like a cannon going off in the barn. As I took a step toward the noise, I ran smack into a wall of flying milk. It was a direct hit. I was slimed from head to toe. While Buckshot was still bucking and making a spectacle of himself for the new babies, I was dripping with warm sticky milk. It was all through my hair and clothes, down through my muck boots to my feet. I wore a bandana around my neck for just such occasions. I wiped as much of the milk off as I could, but there was so much going on in the barn, I didn't want to leave to clean up properly. It was just milk.

Despite Buckshot's hissy fit, our orphans soon settled into their new world. They were split between two large comfy stalls full of fresh bedding, straw and hay. And they had an adoring crowd of staff, volunteers, and friends who would become their servants as these six formerly unwanted little orphans took over the Rescue.

My long ride home that night was uncomfortable and smelly. My milk removal efforts had been inadequate. My scalp itched, my hair was stiff and smelled sour and my socks were still damp. But I was oddly delighted by the episode. I figured the milk shower was a rite of passage providing me fuller entry into the inner hidden delights of the Rescue.

Our motherless babies had to eat every six hours, around the clock. To accomplish this insane schedule, the "Baby Brigade" was started. Rescue staff and volunteers signed up for the 6AM, noon, 6PM, or midnight shifts. The little foals were so bewitching that there were crews of volunteers who drove to the Rescue in the middle of the night to feed them.

We had special powdered milk that approximated mare's milk. It had to be carefully measured and mixed with warm water in six individual buckets, one for each foal. We whipped it forever with a giant whisk until it got to the right consistency. There was no hot running water in the barn, so we used an insta-hot portable propane water heater to heat water from the hose.

An orderly delivery of milk to the foals required a military precision we strove for but failed to achieve. We could not put the milk buckets on the ground because all six starving maniacs would mow each other down to get at them, spilling everything. To avoid this mayhem, we put giant hooks along the fence in their field. This way we could hang the milk buckets off the ground and space them out along the fence. Theoretically, the foals could spread out nicely with one foal to each bucket. But that almost never happened. Much more often, all six would fight over the first bucket put out even as more buckets quickly appeared for them down the fence.

I once tried coaxing Juniper, the tallest foal, to get her head out of an empty bucket and move to a full one. She resisted me like she thought there was some kind of horse cocaine on the bottom of her bucket just beyond her reach. I moved her head to one side so I could see what was so exciting down there. Of course, she jerked her head up, smacking me hard on the chin. I'll never do that again.

We managed to get the foals fed, but they did not live by milk alone. They needed their mothers to protect them, to teach them how to be horses. Since that could not happen, we auditioned mares at the Rescue to see if any of them would accept the foals. I was amazed how many mares were just plain done with kids and really wanted no part of our plans to tie them to the rambunctious, annoying babies. Twister was the exception and the answer to our prayers.

Twister was a beautiful draft cross. Her story was as tragic as the nurse mare foals' own story. Twister was rescued from a well-established and accepted, yet deplorable, program of the pharmaceutical industry. This program produces hormone replacement drugs using the urine of pregnant mares. Twister was bred and, once pregnant, was made to stand still for hours on end while she wore a urinary bladder bag to catch every drop of her urine.

Mares in this program are called PMU mares, short for Pregnant Mare Urine. Not only is this cruel for the mares, their own foals are a nuisance by-product just like the nurse mare foals. They are equally unwanted and their death rate is high. Twister still has a brand on her rump from her days as a PMU Mare. She was urinator number 303.

The six little survivors called to Twister. Maybe they were reminders of her lost babies. Her maternal instinct was super-size and she accepted them all as her own. Twister had adopted Buckshot shortly after his arrival, so they had a few weeks head start on bonding before the other babies came. Buckshot, or Bucksnot, as we nicknamed him, was irritated and crabby at having to share Twister and his once unchallenged place as the Rescue's number one cute baby. Despite this or because of it, Bucksnot was, and remained, Twister's favorite.

Although our babies inhabited a world without their mothers, they did have each other. It was sheer delight to watch them chase each other, springing on their long skinny legs, nipping, bucking, and rearing. They zoomed around their field leaping up like they had Flubber on their hooves (that should date me). They seemed to compete with each other. They would do some odd dance that looked like a fight to the death and then collapse together in a pile of exhaustion, a delightful tangle of heads and legs and tails.

All of us at the Rescue adored these rascals. We treated them like they were puppies. We cuddled them and even napped with them in the field. They sometimes put their heads in our laps and fell asleep. They would come to us whinnying in search of treats and nuzzling us at the fence. They were heart-meltingly, knee-bucklingly cute.

Still, I felt sorry for them because they were orphans. I wanted to give them the love they could never have from their mothers. I wanted to shield them and make everything okay. I did not want them to ever be afraid or insecure. Of course, I was reacting to my own fears for them. They had no clue the odds had been stacked against them. They did not realize they had once been unwanted or that some people thought they were inferior to the big-money foals their mothers were raising. They were the center of attention at the Rescue and their lives were good.

One day, a very well-known trainer who often came to conduct riding clinics at the Rescue observed how friendly and up close we were with the foals. He gave us a stern warning about all the reasons we should not treat them like giant human babies. He said that soon they will think we are foals just like them and will start nipping and charging us like they do each other. He wondered out loud how shocked we were going to be when one of them bites one of our butts. He said we were teaching them not to be afraid of humans. It was hard to hear, but he said we were misleading our babies by allowing them to think all humans were like us. As we knew all too well, lots of humans are shits and the foals should not be taught to think otherwise, especially by us. Not all humans are safe. Not all humans can be trusted. The foals needed to develop a healthy wariness. Sadly, we had to stop treating the 300-pound babies like we were all part of the same species.

Time went by fast and soon six months had passed since the babies arrived. They were getting big and bad and it was time they learned some manners. "Baby School" was born. A few of us volunteers joined together on Saturday mornings with trainers from the Rescue to help teach the foals basic groundwork and respect. They were in high spirits and enjoyed the attention, especially since we had been forced to limit our time with them and could no longer treat them like siblings.

At first, the foals regarded us with curiosity. Were we not their playmates just a while ago? But as we began introducing them to new adventures, they soon figured we actually wanted them to listen to us. We were able to teach all six of them to wear a rope halter and quietly walk on a lead rope without balking or charging ahead or dancing all over. We taught them to halt and back up. We even taught them to walk and trot in a circle around each of us at the end of a long lunge rope. They all learned in different ways and at different speeds, but I was amazed how quickly they picked things up. This band of babies wound their way deeper into my heart every day.

The Rescue had a large outdoor arena that we set up like a carnival spook-house for horses. Horses are prey animals, not predators. That means other animals kill horses. Not being carnivores, horses do not kill other animals for food. They are much more likely to be the food. The flight instinct in horses is extremely strong when confronted with new and strange things. Just as the babies had to learn not every human was safe, they alternately, had to learn that not every scary thing in daily life was going to kill them.

We used Styrofoam "noodles," the kind kids play with at the beach or in the pool, to make one of the obstacles. We tied a few of the noodles to two five-foot poles and set them about three feet apart facing each other. It looked like what you might find at a car wash. The noodles blew in the wind, made noise, and tickled anything that went through them. To us, it looked like we were asking the foals to go through a fun little obstacle. To the foals, it looked like we were asking them to plunge to their death. But with patient encouragement, they all conquered the scary noodles.

We set a large strong square of wood on a log so it would tilt as the foals went over it. We had noisy foil paper that made a racket under hooves. We had low jumps for them to walk over. And at the end, we taught the babies to load up in a horse trailer without drama.

One day, I was leading my then-current favorite, the easy-going Tulip, from the obstacle course back to her field. Out of the corner of my eye, I saw one of the Rescue's four wheelers behind us. It drew closer and, as if on cue, back-fired twice. The ear-splitting noise scared the bejeezus out of me and Tulip. She went straight up and I was looking at her front hooves pawing high in the air over my head. She came down and went up again with more force. I heard a snap and stood holding the lead rope with no Tulip on the other end. It had broken. She had straight up snapped it in two.

Off she went, bucking and rearing, loudly expressing her fear. In my terror, all I could see was her heading flat out for the nearby Interstate. There was an immediate scramble by everyone around to head her off. But instead of racing out toward danger, she headed full speed toward her field. My relief was soon shattered when I saw her gathering herself up to jump the fence. I could see a massive collision of fence, filly, and hard ground. I screamed. But someone had thankfully thought to open the gate to her field. Tulip abruptly changed her mind. Instead of killing herself on the fence, she veered off and cantered through the gate, trotted around her field a bit, head and tail held high, and then settled down to grazing as if absolutely nothing had happened. My heart was racing. I was ready to throw up. I guess peace lasts only as long as nothing backfires—and something always backfires.

Our babies are now beautiful two-year-old teenagers. Yesterday, Daisy and Sundance kept me entertained with nuzzles and horse hugs while I filled the water trough in their field. It is hard to know what is inside a foal, or how it will turn out. Who knows what different bloodlines and environment will produce? These six who, at the very start, had nothing much going for them are turning into great beauties. Food, sunshine, green fields, and doting humans have made spectacular animals out of our six little throwaways.

From the day they first exploded out of the horse trailer, the babies reminded me of the world J.K. Rowling created in her books about Harry Potter. I love her magical beasts, like Dobby the House Elf, Buckbeak the Hippogriff, and Aragog, King of the Arachnids. But my favorite magical creatures are the Thestrals, the invisible skeletal winged horses. The special gift of being able to see a Thestral is offered only to those who have known death. Similarly, the gift of seeing the value and worth of our babies is offered only to those who have known compassion. Without compassion and kindness, you cannot be delighted by our once unwanted babies. Much like Harry Potter who was the "Boy Who Lived," our foals cheated death and became the "Babies Who Lived."

Dawn and her little stowaway, Apollo.

The five adorable "throwaways" from Kentucky.

ANGER

Making Peace with the Rage

There was ample evidence at the Rescue to support the notion that a lot of humans suck. The results of human cruelty were everywhere at the Rescue. You could not escape it. It was enough to piss me off, all day, every day.

Most of the horses at the Rescue, among other illnesses and injuries, had been starved to near collapse. They were described as "neglect cases." I saw raw savagery cloaked in this mild and benign term. You can neglect to brush your teeth. You can neglect to gas up your car. But no one can "neglect" a horse to death. You cannot withhold food from a horse day after day, week after week, month after month until they die, and call it neglect. Just because the cruelty is meted out and endured over time, it is torture, no less than beating a horse to death. Starvation is murder in slow motion. And time after time, the people who owned these horses watched it happen and were okay with it.

Given the severity of the cruelty we saw, how often it happened, and how many people looked the other way to let it continue, I was often in an anger-induced rage. I soon found managing anger was a fundamental survival skill at the Rescue. To stay sane, I had to learn how to deal with my anger. My first lesson came during a public, brutal display of human cruelty.

One hot summer day, the local internet exploded with pictures of a horse dying on a public road in Pennsylvania. A farmer had worked the animal until it collapsed. An eyewitness reported the horse was pulling a wagon over-filled with watermelons. The horse had faltered, too worn-out to continue pulling the wagon. One of the two men riding in the wagon got down and started beating the exhausted horse, forcing him to keep going. He beat the horse until it fell to the ground. The horse could not get up. Still, the man kept kicking the helpless animal as it lay dying. The eyewitness said the animal's tongue was hanging out of its mouth. The horse died, used-up and beaten, on the side of the road.[1]

News of the killing spread like wildfire among horse people. The local news station ran video of the dying horse and interviewed the witness who captured it on camera and called the police. Over forty thousand people shared a Facebook post that included the pictures. People were outraged. I was in the barn petting a horse named Rumor when a visitor to the Rescue told me about it. She was very glad someone had the beating on video because without it, there would be no way to prosecute the man for killing his horse. She said it was not an isolated case. This cruel behavior was apparently not all that unusual. But arrests were rare because there was no proof of the abuse. Now there was proof.

I continued petting Rumor as the visitor told me the story. I loved Rumor and he liked the attention. He had a playfulness about him, a special glint in his eyes. I could not pass him in the field or in a stall without stopping to scratch his forehead and have a chat. I watched Rumor intently nuzzling my palm in hope of treats. As I stroked his neck, I thought of someone laying a hand on him in anger. I thought of someone beating him and kicking him as he lay on the ground unable to get up or defend himself. I thought of his tongue lying on the pavement on the side of the road.

My anger rose up through me from my gut. I was seething. I needed to punch that man who callously worked his horse to death. I wanted to hurt him.

---

1   "Amish man beat 'overburdened' horse until it collapsed, police say," by Peter Holley, The Washington Post, August 6, 2016.

I wanted to kick him on behalf of his horse lying in the road. If he did that in public, what was he doing to his horses in private? I was pissed off to the roots of my hair.

As I was leaving the barn, I saw Taylor. I don't think she was twenty years old yet. She was about 4 feet, 11 inches tall and weighed next to nothing. Taylor was Rescue staff and one of the toughest women I've ever met. We called her Tiny Mighty Taylor. She often gave medicine and administered shots to reluctant horses who had about 1,900 pounds on her. She could dominate the biggest draft horse with a look and the way she carried herself.

I ran to her, excitedly asking if she had heard about the video. She had. "What do you do with the anger?" I blurted out. "I am so mad I can't see straight. How can anyone DO that to a horse? How can we LET someone do that?" I was so mad I was shaking and choking back tears. Taylor was quiet for a minute. Then she told me she only had so much energy in a day. She didn't want to spend a lot of it being angry at something beyond her control that had already happened. She would have that much less energy to do what was within her control for the horses at the Rescue who she could help right now.

And then she said something that changed me. She said the horses could feel the anger inside me. Horses start sizing you up the minute you come into their sight. Horses are prey animals. They are the animals that predators kill and eat. For their own survival, horses need to know immediately if you are friend or foe. Taylor said when I was full of negative energy, my anger made me the enemy. The horses would react with fear and their flight instincts would kick in. They would want to get away from me.

I countered, explaining I was not angry AT them. I was angry FOR them. I was not going to hurt them. I was their friend. I was on their side and wanted to get back at the people who hurt them. Taylor turned to face me. She said that anger was anger. Horses don't know why you are angry, and they don't care. They just want to get away from it. I suddenly felt foolish. Of course, she was right. She went on to say that I had to drop my rage and negativity at the barn door. No matter how well-intentioned it was, I shouldn't bring it inside to the horses

Almost all my life, I have been an advocate. Anger wound me up. Anger had been my constant companion. Anger inspired me to work for reform, to make right that which I thought was wrong. It was the fuel that gave me the energy to persist in the face of overwhelming odds. People I advocated for trusted me because I was angry on their behalf. They liked what they regarded as my passion. But now Taylor was telling me I had to drop it. Now, anger was the enemy.

Taylor's words were hard to hear. But they did clarify my role at the Rescue. It was not to obsess about making sure abusers were punished and atoned for their sins. My job at the Rescue was to comfort, not to get myself all wound up into a dither and frighten the horses. I could be the fierce, avenging angel on the outside, but not at the Rescue. Here, all energy was for the horses who had escaped their tormentors and made it to the Rescue. The abusers did not deserve to take away an ounce of my energy or a minute of my attention from the horses.

We all know old behaviors are tough to change. I needed a mantra or a strong image to focus on, something I could summon when I needed it. It had to be something that kept me from approaching the horses I loved in ways that frighten them.

I thought about Buckbeak, a Hippogriff described in the book *Harry Potter and the Prisoner of Azkaban*. Hippogriffs are magical creatures with the body, back legs, and tail of a horse; the wings and head of an eagle; and they have front legs with long, dangerous talons. As J.K. Rowling describes it in her book, to successfully meet a Hippogriff, you have to first establish a level of mutual respect and trust. You do not want to startle, insult, or challenge a Hippogriff. You have to approach him slowly, with humility, which you demonstrate by bowing to him. Then quietly, you wait for him to make the next move. The Hippogriff has to come to you. If he senses you are dangerous or disrespectful, he will rear up like a stallion and try to slash you. When a Hippogriff accepts you, he will return your bow.

With the image of bowing to a Hippogriff in mind, I focused on being calm and non-threatening when approaching any horse. I intentionally came upon horses in the barn slowly. I silently reached my hand out, my version of bowing. Then I waited. This was not easy as I really wanted to grab their long horse heads with both hands, kiss their noses, scratch their ears and loudly tell them how cute they were.

Coming to the horses in serenity rather than in frenzy worked like magic. When I waited, most horses came toward me, their version of returning a bow. In fact, once I was accepted, the horses put their heads over the stall door and let me pet them. Sometimes, when I lightly scratched their faces, they seemed to nearly doze off with their noses resting on my shoulder. Unlike if your date fell asleep, snoozing in your presence is a high compliment from a horse. It means they regard you as friend not foe and they trust you enough to let their guard down, making themselves vulnerable to attack.

People who are around horses a lot may react to my discovery with a re-sounding "Duuh!" But for me, who often comes roaring into a room or barn, animated, with dramatic gestures and a lot to say, this lesson was revolution-ary. I will never stop raging about the people who do unspeakable things to the animals. But I will save the rage for the ride home. I wanted the horses to know I was not their enemy. I was there to pet them and feed them, not to kill them and eat them.

Because the Rescue was full of horses so badly abused that many were fighting for their lives, you may be thinking it was a sad and miserable place of tragedy and heartbreak, a constant reminder of the darkest places of the human spirit. It was the opposite. The Rescue attracted the most extraordinary people. Volunteers and staff were first responders, like firemen and emergency medical service personnel. They were nurses, service members home from deployment, physical therapists, special education teachers, and veterinary stu-dents. Some had degrees in Equine Management, and many had been riding and caring for horses since they were little tots. The common thread was a mutual delight in saving horses and restoring the frayed human-horse bond. A deep sense of purpose and happiness permeated the Rescue, which at its heart, was a place of joy. At the Rescue, horses, abandoned by everyone else, healed and blossomed into beautiful, proud, glorious animals that could take your breath away.

Yes, we saw the miserable side of human nature. But the Rescue itself was a shining example that humans have great capacity for love, self-sacrifice, tenderness, and devotion. This, plus my growing attachment to the horses, my increasing comradery with staff and volunteers, and everyone's generosity of spirit, left me lighthearted and always coming back to the Rescue.

Photo by Angelina Zepp

There was sometimes tragedy and heartbreak at the Rescue, but at it's core, it was a happy place, full of fun and humor.

Luna, my favorite goat, was left in a field to die when she was a tiny baby. She survived and thrived. The owner of the car, not too put out, said, "Good thing the sun-roof wasn't open!"

Kieran and Damien the ram. Affection has many forms and expressions.

The Mounted Archery Team did exhibition performances at county and local fairs. It was a new level of fun for horse, rider and spectator.

DEATH COMES TO THE RESCUE
A Rite of Passage

I had been at the Rescue for about a year when Merlin came. He was training to be a New York City carriage horse but had a bad accident that severely injured his pelvis, ending his career before it started. Merlin also had Equine Protozoal Myeloencephalitis (EPM). EPM attacks a horse's central nervous system, causing muscle atrophy and loss of balance.

The Rescue staff and the array of other professionals they could call on were brilliant at healing horses. Horses who looked to me like long shots had been cured of diseases, had come back from starvation, and had mentally recovered from abuse. But there were some horses too broken to mend. So it was for our beloved Merlin, no matter how desperately we wanted him to be whole.

Volunteers and staff had been hopeful Merlin could recover from his pelvis injury and that his EPM symptoms could at least be mitigated. Merlin had been stoic through chiropractic procedures, acupuncture, varied diets, and medications. But over time, it became nearly impossible for our beautiful boy to support his own weight. We could no longer let him suffer. So late one summer morning, we gathered from all over the Rescue on one side of the white barn to say goodbye to Merlin who had come to mean so much to so many.

There were nearly twenty of us. Some sat on a pile of gravel that waited to be spread on a nearby dirt road. Some stood in groups. Some stood alone. We were remembering Merlin, each in our own way. As I stood there, my mind floated back to when Merlin first arrived at the Rescue.

He was a huge white Percheron with a powerful, beautifully arched neck, wavy white mane and tail, and a graceful bearing. Although they are officially "Greys," Percherons look white, so I am going to call them white. Merlin was totally white but for the soft, dove grey around his muzzle and his eyes. He looked like he had been done up by a makeup artist, the blue-grey shadow perfectly applied and blended.

There was an air of nobility about Merlin. Even after having rolled in a wet field, caked in mud and smelling suspicious, he still appeared regal and wise. He was young, probably still in his prime. Yet he had a kind old soul and a sense of humor. He retained his classic good looks despite his whimsical forelock that had been cut too short and straight across his forehead. When you looked at him straight on, you could see there was something just a little off in an otherwise perfect face.

My mother used to do the same thing to me when I was little. She would put a small aluminum mixing bowl on my head, cut my hair straight across my forehead and cheerfully call it a "Pixie Cut." Rather than making me cute, I looked like a little tiny soldier with a helmet stuck on my head. It was horrible. I tried always to be sick on the days school pictures were taken. I wondered if Merlin cared that he had a Pixie Cut. Either way, I had a special affinity for him, born of what I perceived to be a mutual affliction.

Along with Merlin's arrival at the Rescue, another white Percheron gelding came to us. He could have been Merlin's twin. His name was Gandalf. Merlin and Gandalf became inseparable. They were a beautiful, if unanticipated, matched set. But, they were not a set for long. Christine bought little Ava when the farm where she lived and everything on it was sold. She was a three-month-old Clydesdale. If there was even the tiniest thing wrong with her, I could not see it. She was so adorable I could not take my eyes off her. And neither could Merlin and Gandalf.

Usually an accommodating mare living at the Rescue would be found to look after an orphaned foal. But Merlin and Gandalf immediately adopted Ava, rarely letting her out of their sight. She could usually be found sandwiched between them or not far away. If they were ever separated, they would call to each other, creating a ruckus. Merlin and Gandalf groomed her and fussed over her and taught her how to be a grown-up horse. They were two great hulking uncles protecting their little ward. We called them, "Ava and the Wizards" as if they were one unit.

Merlin's home was in one of the front fields where he greeted those who passed by his fence. I was once away from the Rescue for several months. Upon my return, I made a beeline directly from my car to Merlin's field. He put his big head over the fence right into my hands. I like to think he had been waiting for me. He lowered his neck to let me hold my cheek to his forehead and soak up his scent, feel the softness of his coat, scratch the base of his ears, and marvel yet again at his size. I had missed him.

When I was very new to the Rescue, I heard the term "companion horse." It referred to a horse not sound enough to ride, but perfectly healthy to be a companion to another horse or human. As much as I loved horses, I could not understand why anyone would want a horse they could not ride. Merlin taught me why. Grooming him, feeding him, and just being with him led me to trust he was not going to hurt me even though at first, I found his size intimidating. Learning to communicate with him through touch was a joy. In turn, he came to trust me, expressing his appreciation for treats and body scratches by nuzzling me and resting his head over my shoulder. We became comfortable with each other. Establishing this agreeable relationship with Merlin made me realize that riding was just one of many ways to interact with a horse. And, that it might not even be the best way.

The week before he died, I remember holding Merlin still while our two vets worked on him. He gently moved his head close to me, offering the opportunity to scratch him. He was calm and patient, nudging me slightly only if I stopped rubbing his forehead.

Our vet did a biopsy of one of his eyes to check for ocular cancer. Merlin looked apprehensive but stood quietly even as the two surgical clamps the vet put on his eyelid softly clinked together when he blinked. Checking his hind-quarters, the vet moved him around a little and I could see he was having a hard time getting his legs aligned and keeping his balance. When he faltered, I instinctively rushed toward his hind end to catch him, like I would a stumbling child. As if I could catch two thousand pounds of falling Merlin. It broke my heart to see him struggling.

The morning Merlin died, we gave him a bath, brushed his white, silky mane and tail and groomed him until he shined. He loved the attention and was in high spirits. I felt all the more like a traitor. He looked mythical, like he could have carried Lady Godiva, or been a super-sized unicorn. We stretched his grooming out as long as we could, knowing that when it was done, we would have to let him go.

By this time, little Ava was with a foster family and no longer at the Rescue, but we could hear Gandalf calling for his buddy from a nearby field. It was heart-wrenching.

The vet gave Merlin an injection in his thick neck, and then another, and the big horse went down. I gasped, my hands flying over my mouth. I don't know what I expected, but it all happened so fast. He was standing with us and, in one second, he was stone-still. He never moved again. His eyes were still open, and I waited for him to blink or twitch or get up, even though I knew he would not. My eyes flooded with tears. In single file, we walked somberly around Merlin's body, each of us saying goodbye to our friend.

It is customary at the Rescue for those who were close to a horse to get a braid made from their mane when they died. I am not sure why I had not asked for one from Merlin. Now that I can no longer see or touch him, I wish I had. Still, I am left with my memories of his massive, graceful body, his head bobbing over the fence, his enthusiasm for food and treats, his gentleness with me and his devotion to Ava and Gandalf. The tears prick at my eyes even as I write this many months later.

I do not know who loved our Merlin before he came to us, whose lives he affected, whose face he nuzzled. Nor do I know if he was mistreated. But I do know he was well-loved at the Rescue. And for a city girl like me who could have never imagined the pleasure of hot, sweet horse breath on her face and did not know the peacefulness that can overcome you in the presence of a magical horse, Merlin was my teacher. He was my wizard. His life and his death have marked me, and I am grateful that I got to know what it was to love him for even the short time I knew him.

It seemed odd to me that a place dedicated to saving lives and restoring hope should be so steeped in death. But death was an unavoidable part of life at the Rescue. Merlin's death was not the only one that day. Dreamer was so new to the Rescue that she was just starting her mandatory thirty days of quarantine to make sure she was not bringing anything contagious into the Rescue. I had not even met Dreamer until the day she died.

She was a stunning brown and white Clydesdale. To my untrained eye, as I watched her in the field, she seemed high-spirited. This made her more attractive to me and made it that much harder to comprehend that she was so sick.

Dreamer had been displaying very odd behavior. The other horses in quarantine were alternating between shunning her and picking on her, a sign that something was wrong. Our vet believed it was a combination of polyneuritis equi and EPM, which made Dreamer a threat to herself and to the other horses. It was not a condition that could be reversed or even treated. She would always be a threat to those around her. To ignore it would be a tragedy in the making and irresponsible. There were no good options for Dreamer.

The other folks at the Rescue had gone back to chores or whatever they had been doing that morning, emotionally exhausted from Merlin's death. It was a small band of four, the vet, two staffers and me, who went to the far-off quarantine field to face what we had to do.

When we brought Dreamer out of the field, the horses still in quarantine nervously trotted back and forth along the fence. They knew something was up. We took her to a small clearing hidden from their view. The vet gave Dreamer the first injection, a tranquilizer, in her neck. But she did not calm down. She was agitated, making it hard for the vet to give her the second, lethal injection. Even after the second shot she did not go down like Merlin had. She reared and paced, turning in circles pulling at the lead rope, dragging the staffer who held her. She just kept going. Why weren't the drugs working? Did she need more? What on earth could we do now?

Finally, she stumbled, dropped to her knees and then down on her side. But her legs kept moving, galloping in the air. It was like she was trying desperately to get somewhere while she still could. I gasped for air and held myself to stop shaking. The barn manager came to me and put her arm around me. "She does not know what she is doing anymore," she said. "It is the symptom of her disease. She is already gone." I believed her, but I could not calm myself. My heart ached for beautiful Dreamer.

At last, her legs quieted and she didn't move. I still held my breath. The vet explained in detail that Dreamer's contortions confirmed her diagnosis and there was no other option but to put her down.

We gently pulled a blue tarp over Dreamer and secured it from the wind with rocks at the edges. She would not be there very long, but I did not want to leave her yet. Even though I could no longer see Dreamer and the tarp did not move, in my mind's eye she was still galloping like she was trying for all she was worth to get home.

My whole body was heavy as I slowly walked back to the main barn, alone, staring at the ground. I wanted to be by myself to process the day. I was rattled and I wanted to think things through. But thinking was not helping. I needed an antidote to my overwhelming sadness. I went to see the six little orphaned nurse mare foals who had come to the Rescue a little while ago.

Daisy was only a week old when she was separated from her mother. Buckshot was less than twenty-four hours old when separated from his mother. Some people would say being orphaned so young left them to start out life behind the eight ball. Maybe, but the foals had no comprehension of it. The babies were happy, spirited, and curious. They rushed the gate when they saw me coming, shamelessly vying for attention. I never tired of watching them chase each other. They sprang on their long spindly legs, testing them out to see what new fun things they could do. They looked at their legs almost as if they were not attached to the rest of their body. They jumped straight up like they had industrial-grade springs on their teeny tiny hooves.

Their antics refreshed my sagging spirits. The feel of their soft little noses and the sound of their high-pitched whinnies made me refocus on the living. Merlin and Dreamer were gone. But these little ones were seizing life with such exuberance, I had no choice but to seize it with them.

Death had come to the Rescue twice that day—one serene, one violent. Both had been acts of kindness. I was drained and exhausted. But I felt I had experienced another essential rite of passage, a testing of mettle where only those who witnessed what I had that day could truly begin to understand the powerful life and death forces at work at the Rescue.

Uncle Merlin and baby Ava. Merlin's "pixie cut" forelock has started to grow out, but you can still see it. My heart warms just looking at his picture.

LEAVING THE RESCUE
Connecting and Letting Go

I knew this day would come. I knew one day he would be adopted and leave the Rescue. It happened one hot August morning. Shelby, the Rescue's in-house trainer, Jessica, a dedicated volunteer, and I left the Rescue early. We were bringing two adopted horses and a colt to their new "forever home" in Pennsylvania. Parting with Felicity, a beautiful white Percheron mare, and baby Apollo was going to be hard. But parting with Atticus, our beloved Belgian, was going to be heart-wrenching.

That's the way it was with the horses we rescued. We fussed over them, calming their fears. We picked their stinky hooves and treated their wounds. We helped them trust humans again. They recovered, and in time, they were adopted. Everyone at the Rescue knew this.

The problem was sometimes you fell in love with them along the way. You hoped they would always be there. You admonished yourself not to get too fond of them, but it just happened. It was their soft eyes, and the way they trotted over to you when you came to their gate. It was when they relaxed in your presence and leaned into you as you groomed them. It was when a horse, who had never in her life had a treat, gingerly took a carrot from your hand. It was when they trusted you when they were scared rather than bolting away from you. That was when they stole your heart.

I always knew Atticus was not mine to keep. But I loved him. And now he was leaving. He was finally healthy, happy, well-trained, and ready for his next adventure. He may have been ready to go, but I was not ready to let him go. I had been part of his fight for survival since he came to the Rescue.

In late October 2015, the Orange County Sheriff's Department raided a farm that became one of the most notorious animal cruelty cases in the Commonwealth of Virginia. When the officers arrived, they found a hellscape of dead horses, mules, cats, dogs and other animals lying all over the 100-acre farm. According to press reports, the officers seized over eighty horses and had to euthanize many more at the scene who were starved and broken beyond all hope. The Rescue was able to take twenty-four draft horses out of that hellhole. Atticus was one of them. [2]

Atticus arrived at the Rescue at dusk. He stumbled down the ramp of the trailer, skinny and caked with dirt. All six of the horses brought from that horrible place that night were in bad shape. Some had been so mistreated that even under our care, they lived only a few more days. Atticus was lucky to have escaped with his life.

Even in the dimming light and in his frightful condition, something about Atticus caught my breath. What I felt from that first fleeting glimpse of him was not pity, as it was with so many of the rescued horses. It wasn't even anger at what he had been made to endure. It was awe. Even ragged, half-starved and apprehensive, Atticus had an air of self-possession about him. He was a survivor. He was alert with a "bring it on" attitude. It was like he knew if he hadn't died yet, he wasn't going to die now.

In the following weeks, I watched him eat and gain strength. As his ribs disappeared, his quirky personality emerged. I was profoundly moved by this horse. I wanted to be part of his recovery. I helped take care of him and early on, I took financial responsibility for him.

---

2   "Update: Peaceable Farm Owner Charged with Animal Cruelty," WVIR NBC29, Charlottesville, Virginia. Posted October 26, 2015; Updated November 9, 2015.

Atticus was a darker color than most of our other Belgians and was there-fore easier to find in a field of Belgians. He had a strong neck with a graceful arch that also made him stand out. His russet-colored coat was like velvet. His flaxen mane and tail provided a stunning contrast. He changed from gaunt to glorious, from cautious to curious, right in front of us. With love, food and time, Atticus developed a grace about him that easily co-existed with his emerging sense of humor and whimsy.

Atticus was missing an eye. But he had a wicked twinkle in the one he had left. He had adapted so well that unless you knew, you would have never guessed he was visually impaired. From his right side, he looked perfect. From his left side, he looked ghostly. At first, I was squeamish about touching his hollow eye socket. But I soon learned he liked to have it scratched. Once I could control my gag reflex and suppress my urge to upchuck, I came to love scratching it for him. He would lean his head into my hand, making sure I could get down deep into the socket's farthest reaches. Not everyone enjoyed watching this. Lots of people were uncomfortable when Atticus and I gleefully demonstrated our eye socket scratching technique.

When Atticus was mentally and physically ready, Shelby began his training. We did not know anything about him before he ended up in that horrible farm in Virginia. Judging by his teeth, we figured he was between thirteen and fif-teen years old, putting him in the prime of his life. Because he was a Belgian, we assumed that at some point he had probably pulled a plow or a carriage, but we could not be sure. Shelby assumed he didn't know anything about being a riding horse and started his training from the beginning.

At first, Atticus resisted her. He crowded into her space, rearing and try-ing to drag her around. Atticus came close to weighing 2,000 pounds. Shelby couldn't have been much over 100. He was so big and she was so small, I wor-ried about her. Nevertheless, it took barely over an hour for her to saddle this giant with attitude and calmly ride him in the round pen. I think he was happy to finally have a job.

Atticus was smart and agile. Shelby went on to teach him low level dressage movements. Who ever heard of a plow/dressage horse? She rode Atticus in a musical pas de deux performance at both the Harrisburg, Pennsylvania and

Timonium, Maryland Horse World Expos with another staff member riding another horse from the Rescue. Their routine was called "Demons," ridden to the song of that name by Imagine Dragons. Atticus, shockingly, was the angel.

Like Shelby, Jessica was in her twenties. She was six feet tall, rail thin and flexible enough to execute a backward somersault dismount off the tallest draft horse. When Jessica and Atticus interacted, their affection for each other was obvious. Jessica liked horses who gave her a hard time. Atticus, opinionated and a trickster, provided enough mischief to keep her entertained. He liked to lick her ears and steal hats off her head. He wiggled around at the three-step mounting block, requiring advanced level gymnastics for her to get on him. He pulled more than one cross-tie out of the barn wall and had a pretty good go at eating the stereo speakers in the indoor arena.

A great team, Jessica and Atticus were invited to join the Gentle Giants Precision Drill Team made up of rescued horses and mules ridden by Rescue staff and volunteers. They performed at county fairs, equestrian clubs and by invitation. They entered dressage competitions, earning ribbons Atticus tried to eat. They were a joy to watch. They beamed in the sunshine of each other's company.

Jessica and I were grateful to Shelby for inviting us to come with her to Atticus's new home. Shelby knew the two of us were having a hard time letting go of our big Belgian buddy. She thought seeing him in his new place with his new people might give us closure. She hoped it would help us find peace with his leaving. Almost all the horses Shelby trained got adopted and left the Rescue. She guarded against letting herself get too close. Even so, I think Shelby, too, was having a hard time now that Atticus was actually leaving.

The morning we left the Rescue, we were in a double crew cab truck, pulling a horse trailer that could comfortably accommodate six big draft horses and what looked like the inventory of a retail tack store. Shelby was driving. I do not know how in this world she maneuvered that thing. There is no way I could have done that. I scraped up my little Prius and obliterated two hubcaps in an underground parking garage before I even made my first car payment. So, when Shelby pulled into a smallish gas station not far into the trip, I thanked God I was not driving the humongous rig with more than 4,000 pounds of shifting horse flesh onboard. But Shelby drove it like it was a Miata. We were gassed up and back on our way before I could hyperventilate.

As we left Maryland, crossing into Pennsylvania, the GPS on Shelby's phone began acting weird. It came up with gibberish that did not look like normal directions. It was August 21, 2017, the day of the total solar eclipse. A kind of heavenly frenzy had gripped the country. I thought all that cosmic activity must surely be creating havoc in outer space, screwing up the GPS. I don't know if we were covered in celestial fairy dust ourselves, but we were all three in a mood to find everything hilarious. Maybe a bit of our laughter was masking the dread of what was in front of us.

Not having a good alternative, we tried to decipher the directions on Shelby's GPS. We soon found ourselves in the heart of a small town. I remember stopping at a red light in the crowded town square. People stared at us. We took up about five or six car lengths. If they looked closely, instead of Clint Eastwood-types driving the big rig, they saw us. I have to admit, we enjoyed their shocked expressions and the stir we were causing. I was in the passenger seat with my feet propped up on the dashboard, head bent, trying not to laugh.

We got through town without incident except for another light that turned red so fast, we had to barrel on through it. Two guys standing on the curb yelled at us. Their outrage was nothing compared to the resulting equine carnage inside the trailer had Shelby slammed on the brakes. I stuck my head out the window to yell back at them, wanting to match cuss word for cuss word, but I pulled back. We didn't need a showdown with the locals while driving a get-away rig that, at full throttle, could go from zero to sixty in about ten minutes.

Along with Atticus, Felicity, a gorgeous white Percheron mare, was also being adopted that day by the same family. She had been my partner horse. She was smart and I enjoyed teaching her things. She was learning how to drink out of the hose when she was adopted.

The same family was also adopting our little Apollo, the stowaway. His story was one of my favorites. You might remember Dawn, the mercy buy who turned out to be pregnant. Instead of being put down, she was well cared for and little Apollo was born. He was big enough to be on his own now and was going to his new home with Atticus and Felicity.

Given the lousy state of our GPS, it wasn't a surprise we overshot the barn we were headed to. We had to turn the big rig around, but we finally arrived safely at our destination. These lucky adopters were ecstatic as we unloaded our precious cargo. They knew how extraordinary our horses were. Atticus was going to be ridden by the teenage daughter and Felicity was for her mother. Apollo was still too young to be ridden. Mother and daughter were visibly delighted and grateful for their good fortune. I started feeling less apprehensive about giving them up.

The new owners had two other horses and a pony. Before we left, we wanted to see how Atticus got along with them. A new horse often got bullied, harassed, or attacked when introduced into an established herd. But when we put him in the field with the other horses, he immediately went full-on killer-Belgian. Rather than letting them challenge him, Atticus was all about a preemptive strike. He showed the other horses who was the biggest and who was going to run the place. Eventually the horses would all get along, but not that day. We took Atticus out of that field and put him in another one with Felicity and Apollo. After rolling and running around, he settled down like he had always lived there.

The land was lush and green and beautiful. There was a very old barn being renovated. It had a hay loft with a spectacular view from which Jessica and I could watch our three friends adjusting to their new home. Shelby was done with the paperwork for the adoptions all too soon. We hung around for a while, but it became clear there was no real reason for us to stay. Sooner than I was ready, I said goodbye. Jessica and I both stole a look over our shoulders as we left. It was probably the last time we would ever see Atticus, Felicity and Apollo. It was certainly the last time we would see them as we knew them that day.

Back on the road, two tons lighter and our mission accomplished, we realized we had not eaten real food all day. The not inconsiderable weekly snack purchase for volunteers at the Rescue had been accidently left in the back seat of the truck. Though we had raided it throughout the day, it was down to only things we didn't like. In addition to being starved, we all had to go to the bathroom. So of course, we got stuck behind a farmer on a tractor going five miles per hour down a narrow country road.

We were unable to pass or get around him. He was wearing headphones and was oblivious to us bearing down on him. Embracing our fate, we could only laugh at ourselves. But the more we laughed, the more we had to pee, the more miserable we were.

The farmer eventually pulled off the road. But Shelby's GPS was still bewitched. While the rest of the world was reveling in the glorious beauty of Mother Nature showing off through the total eclipse of the sun, our GPS was now just screwing with us. It directed us into a neighborhood cemetery. Once we found our way out of there, it took us to what looked like the overflow section of the local dump. When it took us to a country lane not much more than an overgrown path, we abandoned it. We could do better navigating blindfolded.

We finally came to an intersection Shelby recognized. Now, where to eat? Even with full bladders and empty stomachs, Shelby and Jessica were picky about where to stop. I didn't care. I was ready to eat my boots, if I didn't pee in them first. They finally agreed on Checkers, but Shelby had to gun our unwieldy rig across a four-lane highway to get there. We had not chosen wisely. The Checkers bathroom entrance was on the outside of the building and it only accommodated one at a time. We took turns waiting outside. It started to rain.

It was late when we finally got back to the Rescue. Jessica had missed a riding lesson, Shelby had many chores yet to do, and I had a long ride home. But it had been an important day. Together, we had gotten lost, found our way back, laughed and discovered peace in letting Atticus go. Those connections made for a rare shared experience.

Shelby had been through this all before, but for Jessica, the adoptions completed a circle. She had now experienced all the stages of a horse's journey through the Rescue. Unlike me, she had been brave enough to go with

Christine to the New Holland Auction. She had seen the meat men buying live horses priced by the pound destined to be slaughtered and eaten. She had seen the miserable condition these horses were in. She had felt the pain of leaving behind the ones that could not be rescued. She had thrown herself into the care and recovery of the ones we could save. Today, she had seen the result of that love and care. Our horses, having been restored in both body and spirit, were now with a family who would love them.

Still, the loss of Atticus cut deep. Jessica did not know it then, but in a while, she would find a place in her heart for another Gentle Giant. Her name would be Vera and she would be a whole new chapter in Jessica's story.

I too found other horses to dote on. But once in a while when I drive up the Rescue's long driveway, I stop at Atticus's field even though I know he will not be there. What I feel now is not so much the emptiness of loss but the fullness of having had this outsized horse in my heart. I once felt only the pinch of being left with less. Now I know Atticus expanded my capacity to accommodate what was demanded of me if I was to have these Giants in my life. I expected it to be hard when they died. I did not know it would be so hard when they thrived. Having loved my big boy and having let him go was to experience yet another rite of passage at the Rescue. Atticus and his wondrous hollow eye socket will be with me always. A girl can never forget her first one-eyed Belgian.

When Atticus was ready mentally and physically, Shelby began his training. He was so big and she was so small, I worried about her.

Jessica and Atticus were a great team. They entered dressage competitions winning ribbons Atticus tried to eat. Look closely, and you can see his wondrous eye socket.

Atticus on the left, Felicity on the right and me in the middle just before we loaded up to leave the Rescue. Saying goodbye to these two was hard.

TONKA
Turning the Corner

One morning, I arrived at the Rescue later than I expected. I parked my little silver Prius between two big muddy crew cab trucks with gun racks, job boxes, and random machinery poking out of their beds. I hurriedly slipped out of my strappy sandals, pulled on my muck boots, and fiddled with my hair to get it on top of my head, out of my way. I was tying a faded bandana around my forehead to keep sweat out of my eyes when I came upon two Rescue staff talking excitedly about a new horse named Tonka who had arrived that morning. He was up in the rehabilitation barn ("rehab") where horses who need specialty medical procedures or intensive care were kept.

Apparently, a concerned neighbor had called The York County Pennsylvania Society for the Prevention of Cruelty to Animals (SPCA) about a horse in a nearby field who looked to be in bad shape. When the owner of the horse was confronted, she agreed to give the horse up. The SPCA contacted the Rescue. Rescue staff immediately got the horse from Pennsylvania, and brought the poor thing back to the Rescue.

I walked up the hill to rehab, anxious to check out Tonka before I got caught up in daily chores. As I rounded the corner of the barn, I caught sight of a big white head leaning out of the end stall. Before I got right up to the stall door, I stopped short. There he was, the tallest horse I had ever seen in my life. In a barn built to accommodate huge horses, his ears nearly grazed the light fixture hanging from the beam high up in the ceiling.

Distracted by his height, it took me a second to focus on his condition. I muffled a gasp. He was a skeleton. I had seen starvation cases at the Rescue before but nothing like this. I don't know how he was standing up. His flesh was drawn so tightly over his bones I was sure they would pierce his skin. His hip bones stuck out like they were not part of the rest of his body. I could clearly see each individual rib. As I stared at Tonka, it was as if the picture of a horse skeleton hanging in the volunteer lounge was staring back at me.

I winced because it hurt to look at him. But I couldn't stop looking. I left the rehab barn afraid I was going to be sick. Tripping down the hill back to the main barn, I fought back tears. Over the years, I have been largely able to curb crying in public. But my tears came now. Tears of shock. Tears of misery. Tears of rage. How could a human being do this to a horse? How could you watch your horse starve to death? It was beyond anything I could comprehend. Someone should have to pay. In a civilized society, this meanness and cruelty should not go unpunished.

I threw myself into the physical work of the farm. But there wasn't enough shit to shovel, feed to haul, or hay bales to unload to dull my jagged anger. I wanted to avenge Tonka. I could not shake his emaciated image.

At the end of the day I went back to rehab, exhausted from ranting and banging things around. The other horses in the barn had been let out into their field for the night. Only Tonka and Erica, the Rescue's Equine Manager, were there. Tonka had been taken out of his stall and was standing in the wide aisle running down the middle of the barn. I got a good look at him. He was a white Percheron gelding, although between the raw nasty sores and the black stuff that looked and felt like tar all in his hair, it was hard to believe he had ever been white. His long neck looked like it had been hollowed out with an ice cream scoop. His mane that hung past his knees was more like a ghostly tattered shroud than hair. He was holding up his left front foot trying not to put weight on it.

Standing close to this abused horse in the calm of the barn, the anger toward his owners that had consumed me all afternoon gave way to an overwhelming tenderness. I slowly approached Tonka, no longer seething with righteous rage. My anger, even if on his behalf, would do him no good now. He raised his head. I lightly touched his cheek with my fingertips, afraid his skin might disintegrate. I moved a bit closer and gently put my whole hand on his cheek. I wanted in one movement to wash away his pain. I scratched his forehead. I scratched his ears. He leaned in and I noticed his eyes—oh my God, his deep brown eyes. I did not see anger in his eyes, only a softness that made me ashamed to be part of the species who did this to him. In searching Tonka's eyes, I felt something pass between me and this horse who had so little left.

By now, everyone else had gone home. The Rescue was sinking into the stillness of nightfall. I hung around not wanting to leave. I cradled Tonka's head and petted his nose. Erica showed me the special alfalfa I could slowly hand-feed him. We had to be careful what we fed him, as well as how much and how fast. When a horse has been starving for as long as Tonka had, getting it wrong could be fatal. His systems had basically shut down. If we fed him more than he could process in his fragile state, his kidneys could fail and he could die.

I kept him distracted with soft pets, a comforting voice, and alfalfa while Erica began slowly picking the dirt and sticky stuff out of his mane. Erica was almost eight months pregnant, swollen and near bursting with life. Tonka, emaciated, was fighting for his. My throat tightened with emotion as I watched her carefully untangle the worst of the matts in Tonka's mane. I could not help but see what was unfolding in front of me. Erica was carrying the life force of birth. Tonka, who had been rescued from certain death, was being given the chance of rebirth. Corny? Maybe, but that was what I felt as Erica and I quietly began saving Tonka.

Erica kept working on the stiff, tarry crud covering his body, but it was stubborn. Only a bath could get rid of it. She got out the hose and the shampoo. Luckily, Tonka was not afraid of the water and did not object to a bath. She gently and methodically stroked him, washing away the misery of his old life along with the dirt and scum. I watched it all cling to the drain in the middle of the barn floor for a second and then disappear out of sight, gone forever. He was with us now.

Once he was as clean as we could get him, Erica's attention turned to the foot Tonka had been protecting. We knew his hoof had been punctured. We would have to wait for an x-ray to see if his bone had been punctured too. We already knew his hoof was infected. It would have to be cleaned and dressed. We were pretty sure he could not support himself on only three legs so we slowly moved him closer to the wall so he could lean on it for support while Erica worked on his hoof. Tonka trusted her, giving her his sore hoof when she asked for it. Or maybe he was just too weak to object. She thoroughly cleaned it out and packed gel antibiotic deep into the puncture wound. She covered the whole thing with thick gauze and wrapped his enormous hoof with pink vet wrap.

Tonka was so tall that his back was over both our heads. I stood by him on one side and threw a blanket over his back to Erica on his other side. It was a struggle, but together, we got the warm blanket over him and secured with clips. We tucked him in for his first night out of the hell hole. He was clean, cared for, and loved. He was in a big stall of fluffy soft bedding. He had plenty of fresh water, hay, alfalfa, and a pan with some grain mash complete with antibiotics and painkillers. We had given him the best chance to survive we knew how. But as we turned off the barn lights, we knew his condition was dire; he still might not make it through the night. It was up to Tonka now.

When I got home, I checked Facebook. The Rescue had posted pictures of Tonka arriving at the Rescue. They were hard to look at and people reacted with shock and anger. Most of the comments were encouraging and touching. But one read something like, "If you have an ounce of humanity, for God's sake put that horse down." Reading it stung like a slap in the face. But looking again at the pictures of him when he first arrived, a filthy dirty horse skeleton standing in our barn, I could understand the comment. Could it be there actually was no hope for Tonka? Were we being cruel by trying to save him? Were we just a well-intentioned continuation of his abuse? Was he better off dead?

I seriously thought about the Facebook comment. I had seen many hard decisions made at the Rescue. I did not think they wanted to try saving Tonka just so we could all feel good. A starvation case as severe as Tonka's required a huge commitment of staff and volunteer time and money. It was risky and a long shot at best. Every horse required tough decisions. In the end, I totally trusted the people at the Rescue to know the right way. I respected the commenter's view, but I went to bed proud of what we had done. The Rescue staff saw something in Tonka and so had I. Maybe I am a flakey do-gooder cupcake with no common sense, but what I saw when I looked into Tonka's eyes was not a horse ready to give up.

Tonka did not die that night, or the next or the next. He kept on living and eating and getting stronger. Our incredible vet came to see him often. With her mobile unit, she x-rayed his punctured hoof. His bone had been punctured but was not infected. That was good news for Tonka. If he didn't have to fight off a bone infection, Tonka's wounded hoof had a better chance of healing. Still, the puncture would require constant attention. Fortunately, the Rescue had two remarkably talented and ingenious farriers who did not mind dealing with 2,000-pound draft horses. Our Dream Team fashioned a metal shoe for Tonka that could open and close. It had a rim secured around the outside edge of Tonka's hoof, and a flat metal platform that covered the bottom of his hoof. It could be screwed on and off, giving relatively easy access to the wounded hoof, but provided maximum protection from dirt and further infection. It also made it easier to change his dressing every day. With the use of this contraption, called a hospital shoe, Tonka's hoof began healing.

Volunteers who helped care for Tonka posted photos of his progress on Facebook and Tonka soon became the darling of the Rescue. The negative comments all but disappeared and brilliant words of encouragement poured in from all over the country and the world. I started feeling better about human nature. My belief in the goodness of mankind had taken a hit seeing what had been done to Tonka. The heartfelt words of encouragement from people who had never met any of us were like a cool soothing salve.

The weeks went by and Tonka got better and better. He started walking on his injured hoof. He nickered softly as though thanking us when we approached him with food. He loved attention and stood near the fence offering his giant head for petting and admiration for as long as anyone would love him up. His soft eyes were mesmerizing. We were all captivated. At some time in Tonka's life, he had known real human kindness. It made his situation all the more incomprehensible. What the hell had gone so wrong?

Not long after his arrival, Tonka became obsessed with one of his stable-mates in the rehab barn. Madison was a beautiful white Percheron mare, and he was completely taken with her. He wanted to be near her whenever possible. If he couldn't be in the field with her, he maneuvered himself so he could at least see her from his stall. Both being white Percherons, they had a lot in common, but primarily, it was the pain they had suffered.

Madison had been a carriage horse in New York City. She came to the Rescue extremely lame. The sinews around her hooves were inflamed and the inner wall of her hoof bone was badly worn. She was sick and could barely stand. Like Tonka, the Rescue had Madison fitted with custom shoes to relieve her hoof pain. She had been in the rehab barn for many months receiving diligent care, but her recovery had been touch and go. I remember we used to slowly walk her to the indoor arena at night where the ground was soft and lying down was more comfortable for her. Her shoes eventually worked and she started making steady progress. By the time Tonka came, she was well on her way to recovery. Not long after Tonka arrived, the vet determined our sweet Madison was sound again and cleared her to begin training as a saddle horse. I never in a million years thought she would make a full recovery, let alone ever be able to be ridden.

I think Madison encouraged Tonka. Maybe she communicated to him that he was in a good place now and could count on us not to give up on him, like we had not given up on her. Whether or not she inspired Tonka, I know Madison's recovery inspired me to keep believing that even seemingly hopeless cases could be successful.

In time, Tonka's bones became less pronounced and his rear end looked less like two craters. As he began trusting that he could count on four square meals a day with snacks, his personality began to emerge. When he had more energy than it took to merely survive, he started acting like the big horse he was. Paula, a staffer particularly fond of Tonka who spent a lot of time wrapping his punctured hoof and monitoring his feed, wrote on her Facebook page:

"Oh my heart. Tonka just came trotting up through the rehab sac lot. Even better, he got pushy and I had to yell at him and chase him away. I could not be more pleased."

Tonka got strong enough to stand for the farriers and have his feet worked on. They cleaned and trimmed all four of his hooves. When they were done, I took him for a walk. It took a few steps for him to get used to the feel of his newly trimmed hooves, but he soon settled into my pace and walked beside me like an angel. I was thrilled he was no longer limping. We set off down the path just outside the rehab barn.

All was well until we turned around. I was figuring we would walk a little further down the other side of the barn door before going back to his stall. But Tonka was already making the turn into the barn. I pulled lightly on the lead rope, assuming he would change course and follow me. Nope. He was going back into the barn. I told him to stop. Nothing. I pulled harder on the lead rope. Still nothing. By now he was almost totally in the barn while I was still outside. I tried to nudge his butt over so I could at least squeeze between him and the barn wall to get ahead of him. Nothing. It was like trying to move my garage. I foolishly thought I could still get control of him until I felt fire in the palm of my hand. It was the long lead rope whizzing through my fingers despite my tight grip. If I didn't let go, I was going to burn my hand more or slam into the side of the barn. I let go. Off went Tonka without me.

I was truly shocked. Not at getting dragged, but at getting dragged by Tonka! What happened to the horse who barely had the strength to stand up? Where was my weak, sweet, vulnerable boy who did everything I asked? When did he get a mind of his own or the strength to act on it? When did I lose control?

Tonka stopped in the middle of the barn, and I scrambled after him. He stood quietly while I recovered the lead rope. I stupidly thought he was sorry that he had drug me. But then, he got a whiff of his dinner that had been put in his stall while we were out. His stall door was open. The whole thing started over. Tonka headed for his dinner as if I wasn't there. The lead rope went smoking through my raw hand again. Same choice, get drug into the wall or let go. For the second time in five minutes, I let go. When I caught up with him, he was happily munching his mash, oblivious to the distress he had caused me. I just stared at him.

I felt abandoned. Where was fragile Tonka who would take a few steps and stop so politely? In my heart I knew this was what we had all been praying would happen. He probably had a 3,000-pound personality to go with what was surely going to be a 3,000-pound body. He was named after a series of trucks and earthmoving equipment, for God's sake! (Even if they were just toys.)

Paula considered every moment a teachable moment. She had seen what happened. She was always telling me I needed to be tougher with the horses. I needed to act like a boss mare, like I was calling the shots and the horses' job was to follow my lead. She told me I should have turned Tonka around, marched him right out of the barn and made him re-enter together with me like a civilized horse. I grimaced and said I did not want to hurt him by making him cross his legs over each other to turn around in the barn. Exasperated, she explained that no matter the tenderness I felt for him and what he had lived through, I had to stop coddling him or he was going to run all over me. Tonka had turned a corner. It was important for my ability to handle him, that I turn that corner too. I had to stop treating him like he was a frail pony.

Christine says horses do not want to be thought of as victims when they are with us at the Rescue. They have fallen on hard times but that does not define who they were or who they will be. She thought it was especially true with Tonka. He had probably been strong, proud, and loved a lot longer than he had been abandoned, weak, and needy. She said we all had to stop treating him as if he was still fragile. It was easy to see I was particularly guilty of this. I was late to the idea that Tonka had to be handled like he was a strong giant of a horse who needed to know what was expected of him and what behavior was not ok. This was not just for Tonka's sake; it was for our own safety. If we didn't see how powerful he was going to be and learn how to control him now, he was going to be dangerous. To remind ourselves, we started calling him Sir Tonka.

When I look back on the first day Sir Tonka came to us, I remember putting my hand on his face wanting to instantly relieve his pain and heal him. It was not happening in the blink of an eye like I wanted, but it was happening. It would take time and the combined efforts of everyone—staff, volunteers, vets, farriers, and online supporters—to pull it off. But Sir Tonka was winning the fight for his life. As he embraced his life and grew bolder, he was showing me there was more to rescuing a horse than feeding and loving him when he was weak. I needed to grow with him and adapt to the horse he was becoming and would be. I had to go on his journey alongside him or I would get left behind, slammed into the side of the barn or forced to let go of the horse I cared so much about.

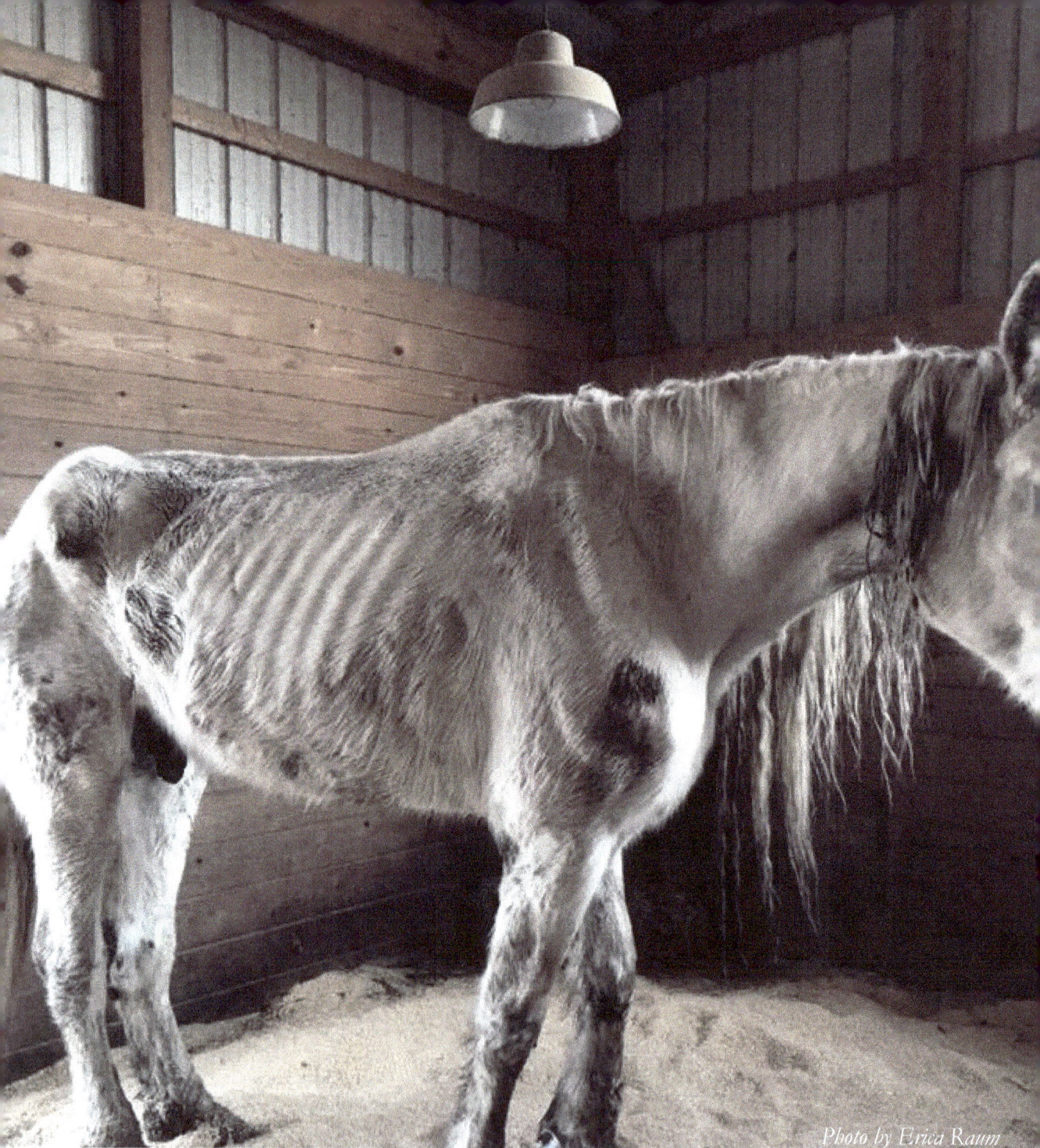

Tonka the day he came to the Rescue. I had seen starvation cases at the Rescue before, but nothing like this.

Tonka was obsessed with Madison.

Tonka restored.

LIFE AT THE RESCUE
Embracing the Creative Chaos

My trip to the Rescue was an inspiring ride past some of our country's most iconic historical landmarks. Alan and I lived on the fringe of the old historic part of the city of Alexandria, Virginia that George Washington famously mapped out when he was a young surveyor. Old Town Alexandria was once a busy port on the Potomac River. It had played an outsized role in both the Revolutionary War and the Civil War. I got to snake my way through two centuries of Colonial and Early American history just getting out of Old Town and onto the George Washington Parkway heading north to Maryland.

The Parkway, as it is called, ran along the Potomac River for quite a while past sailing marinas and the Reagan Washington National Airport. Just across the Potomac, I could see the U.S. Capitol where I worked for many years. Moving farther up the Potomac, I passed the Jefferson Memorial, the Washington Monument, the Lincoln Memorial, and the Kennedy Center for the Performing Arts. The old spires of Georgetown University, several boat launches and the National Cathedral were also visible on the far bank of the river. If I was lucky, I could see the Georgetown Crew Team out practicing. To my left, I could see parts of the Arlington National Cemetery.

In the space of a few minutes, I could hear the Washington, D.C. Metro passing on the left as it came above ground for a while, planes flying low overhead, taking off from the airport, and cars honking on the road, all as I looked at water taxis, motorboats, canoes and sailboats on the Potomac River to my right.

The Parkway ran into I-495 which then merged into I-270, making the second part of the trip a hurried blur of suburban freeway. Luckily, I was going out of town against all the traffic heading into town and rarely got stuck in the notorious D.C. traffic jams. Leaving the freeway, I came to a multi-lane highway running past a shopping center and a Maryland subdivision crowded with newly built "McMansions."

Before long, the highway narrowed back to the two-lane country road it had been before the exurbs encroached. I passed cornfields, cows, used tractors and cars for sale on the side of the road, and a large John Deere farm machinery distributor. In the summer, there was a farmer's market where, if I had time, I stopped for homemade cookies, fresh local peaches, and whatever other fresh produce they had that day. But my favorite item was their caramel popcorn with Old Bay seasoning. Old Bay is very spicy and usually used with steamed crabs and other seafood, but its salty sting mixed with caramel was a combo I could not get enough of. By the time I got to the Rescue, I would have finished the entire bag, my lips tingling from the Old Bay and the steering wheel a sticky mess.

I was happy to spend the whole hour and a half ride in my own head, letting my mind just wander, but by the time I hit the Maryland countryside, I was often ready for songs I could sing along to at the top of my lungs. One of my favorite sing-a-long CDs was Miranda Lambert's Platinum.

But once I turned off the road onto the Rescue's long gravel driveway, everything going on in the car stopped. I put all the car windows down, no matter the weather. I breathed deeply. I let whatever came with me from the city blow away. I gave myself over to whatever was waiting for me at the Rescue.

Once, I arrived on Castration Day. Sundance, Gunsmoke, and Buckshot were about six months old by then and had just been gelded. They were sedated and resting comfortably. Being a coward, I was relieved to have missed the vet working on the boys. I had known them since they were little ones, just a few weeks old. The thought of a knife cutting into those sweet tender babies was horrifying.

I did, however, get there in time to see Ferguson, our lovely sheep, go under the knife. It would be easier for me to watch Fergie because I did not know him like I knew the colts. But Fergie was Tara's favorite. Tara had practically grown up at the Rescue. She was a fixture, helping out there since she was a little girl. She was quite nervous for her friend. Tara sat in Fergie's stall cradling his head in her lap while the vet sedated him. She held him throughout the whole ordeal. Sedation is a wonderful thing. Fergie barely knew what clipped him.

The barn was quiet as a few of us watched intently. Our vet was quick and efficient. But at the end of the procedure, she realized she didn't have a container to put Fergie's testicles in. The four of us watching the operation quickly searched for something suitable. Someone spied an empty Starbucks cup. It was the clear kind made for specialty drinks. At first, we hesitated. It did not seem sufficiently respectful for the occasion. But the vet was still holding Fergie's testicles and we could not immediately find anything better in the tidy barn. So the vet carefully slid Fergie's testicles into the Starbucks Grande cup. They filled the container perfectly, right up to the clear domed lid designed to accommodate whipped cream.

Maybe it was because we were all women in the barn on Fergie's big day, but we thought the "Fergie Frappuccino" proudly displaying the beautiful Starbucks Mermaid logo was knee-bucklingly hilarious. We broke what had been somber silence when we busted out laughing and couldn't stop. Had there been men with us, perhaps we would not have laughed until we hung on the stall doors for support. If the vet needed to take Fergie's testicles back to her clinic, I hoped she did not put the Starbucks cup in her van's dashboard cup holder. It looked way too much like a Caramel Macchiato, which I will never see the same way again.

On another day, I entered the empty barn to find a large, thick pile of some kind of material on the floor. The tips of a nice pair of shoes peeked out from underneath. It looked as if the Wicked Witch of the West had melted right there on our barn floor, leaving nothing but her cloak and shoes behind. I half expected to see her black pointy hat close by, and flying monkeys swooping through the barn in chevron formation.

I warily circled the pile. I poked it with my toe. It didn't seem to be alive but neither did it seem to be dead. While I pondered, someone I had never seen before came into the barn. "What on earth is this?" I asked her, pointing to the pile on the floor. She smiled, noting my bewilderment, and told me the mysterious pile was raw wool sheared and gathered that morning from all the sheep on the farm. The shoes were the sheep shearer's street shoes and she was the sheep shearer.

I took a walk around the Rescue to check out the sheep. I could see the poor things were agitated. They seemed embarrassed and indignant at being left naked. It was a hot day and they were surely more comfortable without all their wool, but they did not regard any of us with gratitude. They looked odd to me. Features that were barely noticeable before the shearing were now dominant. Before, their necks, heads, and legs had all but disappeared into the fullness of their wool coats. They were like overgrown Chia Pets. Now, it was backwards. They were all spindly long legs, skinny necks, and heads. The sheep had never been exactly cuddly, keeping their distance from most humans, but now they kept a whole lot of yardage between themselves and all of us. What was done for their own good just seemed to piss them off.

If the sheep were uneasy that day, Millie the pig was about to become homicidal. The sheep shearing lady was also the pig toenail-clipping lady. Millie was a pot-bellied pig. She weighed about 225 pounds. She had free run of the Rescue, but her fat belly dragged on the ground and hindered how fast or how far she could go. Rarely venturing out of the barn, Millie liked to burrow deep into the hay in the horse stalls so you could not see her. If you were unlucky enough to stumble over her, she would let out a shriek that shot up your spine leaving you clutching your heart. She roamed the barn snuffling and complaining. The horses were pretty much used to her movements and her noises, but I was not. Millie and I had history.

One afternoon I was bent over cleaning out a hind hoof of one of our big Belgian horses named Zeke. His hoof was the size of a satellite dish and heavy as a cannonball. I had seen Millie waddling in and out of a few empty stalls searching for dropped grain and other tidbits. But, concentrating hard on Zeke's hoof, I kind of forgot about her. Until something displeased her. She belted out a scream that penetrated my central nervous system. Still holding Zeke's hind leg, I jerked in surprise, knocking myself in the head with his giant hoof. Well, maybe it was just a tap on my forehead with his hoof, but I have had mixed feelings about Millie ever since.

The toenail-clipping lady was there because Millie hated to have her toenails cut. She always took evasive action. Because she behaved so badly when approached with the clippers, her nails had not been done in some time. Now the expert had been called in. There would be no tolerating her antics today.

Apparently, pigs cannot be sedated. I had not known that and was not happy to hear it. They get what's called malignant hyperthermia. Sedatives make them overheat to the point their lives are at risk. I was apprehensive about how we were going to deal with our squealing, wriggling, muddy, extremely grumpy pig, full-on awake. There were five of us ready to handle Millie. That did not seem near enough people to contain her. But with a bit of coordination, we were able to wrangle her into the corner of a stall. We packed hay around her so she wouldn't hurt herself when she struggled. We rolled up a towel for her to bite on so she didn't bite on us. The noises she made were not of this world.

Four of us sort of laid on her, but she still managed to bump us around pretty good. The pig nail-cutting lady was quite fit. She was able to straddle Millie while wielding something that looked like a hedge clipper. She had several different types of tools. I handed them to her when she needed them as best I could while still trying to keep Millie pinned down. She repositioned herself a lot, getting the best angle and the most leverage for each one of Millie's toenails. As she moved around, thick toenail missiles shot out from her clippers, hitting the walls of the stall. The more she clipped, the harder Millie thrashed.

I was curious what would motivate someone to choose this line of work. Between Millie's howls, I asked her if she liked doing this for a living. She said she much preferred it to the desk job she had for twenty years. Here she was, sweating in the heat, bent so far over she was working nearly upside down, brandishing an array of sharp, heavy tools with a murderous, giant pig wailing between her legs. That must have been one heinous desk job!

We all survived Millie's piggy-pedi. Having exhausted her deep reservoir of badassary, she sulked for the rest of the day.

I did not usually go to the Rescue on Saturdays, but Christine had started a "Yoga for Riders" class on Saturday afternoons in the barn's second floor multipurpose room that I wanted to check out. I got to the Rescue well before the yoga session started in order to hang out and have quality time with the horses in the barn. It didn't matter which horses were there. I enjoyed them all. Time spent with any of them was a joy.

In the summer, some horses were in the barn to escape the crazy heat. Some, especially the white ones, were in the barn to avoid getting blistering sunburns. Some had eye conditions that were aggravated by the blazing sun. But some horses were in the barn because they needed to be around people. Somewhere in their past, something bad had happened to them that frayed the human-horse relationship. Like physical wounds, their emotional wounds needed time and the right environment to heal.

One such case was a Belgian mare named Nola. An animal welfare group in Louisiana was alerted to a situation where several horses, caught in high flood waters, were unable to get to safe ground. The horses were struggling and would not survive without help. When they led a rescue operation that succeeded in saving the horses, the Rescue was happy to take Nola.

When Nola got to us, she was scrawny and bit-up. She had a hard time adjusting to her new life. Afraid of everything, she stood back in her stall as far away from people as she could get. She ate, but she could not gain weight. Some speculated she had picked up parasites in the swamp that were eating her up from the inside. Over time, medication conquered the parasites, but Nola would still not engage with people. She wasn't hostile or dangerous, as some fearful horses can be. She was just so very sad.

I am a type A, extroverted personality through and through. Standing quietly anywhere for anything is hard. I am a twitcher, always a foot or a leg moving, pacing, fingers drumming. To me, there is comfort in motion. Doing is better than not doing. But Nola did not respond well to big motions or loud sounds. She was not drawn in by my colorful denunciations of whatever jackass left her in the swamp. I wanted so much to pet and reassure her, but I knew I would have to change my approach. I began learning from Nola that I needed to slow down, be still, shut up, and listen.

At first, I just stood by her stall where she could see me. After a few sessions, she turned her head my way. I asked nothing of her, but with more time, she would take a step toward me. Curiosity about carrots got the best of her and one day, feet planted in case she had to retreat, she stretched her neck way out and warily took the offering from my hand. The tickle of her soft nose on my palm was a thrill.

Many of us quietly worked with Nola. Her progress delighted us all. She was now poking her head out when she heard voices rather than retreating into the darkness of her stall. Lena, our vivacious Volunteer Coordinator, asked if I could spend time with Nola before the yoga class. Lena was always upbeat. I liked being around her and there was not much she could have asked me to do that I wouldn't do. I more than cheerfully obliged her request. I took a bucket of grooming supplies into Nola's stall and spent a good hour picking out her hooves, brushing her light copper color coat, and combing out her Barbie doll wavy blonde mane and tail. She let me hold her head and lightly scratch her face. She closed her eyes and rested her head on my shoulder. Together, we had found a way to comfort each other.

The yoga class was an hour of calm, slow movements. I felt good after the session. Walking through the barn back to my car, I saw Zeke. Because the big Belgian was one of my favorites, I had to stop to see what was going on. Sam, a quiet, calm Rescue staffer, was treating Zeke's feet. Sam was a young woman of few words who missed nothing. She was methodical and efficient with her movements. She was wonderful at tending horse injuries and administering medicines. Whenever I saw her, I knew something interesting would be going on. Sam had Zeke tied in the center aisle of the barn and was tending him by herself. Sometimes Zeke could get to dancing around when people were working with his hooves so, hoping to be helpful, I held his head to distract him while Sam completed his complicated treatment.

Zeke came from the New Holland Auction where Christine out-bid the foreign slaughterhouse buyers, saving him from a nasty death. Inexplicably, the shoes on Zeke's two front hooves had been nailed, not into his outer hoof wall where it doesn't hurt, but right into his hoof. He was in great pain. As soon he got to the Rescue, our farriers removed his shoes. His front hooves were all infected and a terrible mess. Our vet treated the infections and for a while, Zeke made progress. But eventually the infection returned to both hooves. This time the vet cut out the infected part of the hoof. Our two clever farriers conferred with a few others in the business and fashioned two very special shoes. They were a lot like the special shoe made for Tonka. They had a removable bottom plate for easy access to Zeke's hoof. This was important because three times a day, we irrigated his hooves with an iodine mixture, changed the dressing, and re-packed it. There was also a top part of the shoe that screwed into the bottom plate to hold Zeke's hoof together. The vet said it would take a year for his hooves to grow back and for him to heal. His cut out, misshapen hooves looked appalling to me and a year sounded like forever. But I had faith in the assembled wisdom and talent Christine could call on. I did not waver in my belief that we could be successful and Zeke would be just fine.

Zeke's mane was clipped (roached) so it was just an outline of his powerful neck. He was so big and beautiful that if a superhero was looking for a horse, they would pick Zeke. As I held him for Sam, I ran my fingernails lightly down his neck and back and over his butt. He loved that. Even though his hooves were getting irrigated with iodine, he was relaxed. He dropped his head over my shoulder, wiggled his lips, and I swear he cuddled. I loved this guy. I was such a sucker for Belgians.

Ginger, a very vocal mule, was in one of the stalls near us. She was only there waiting for her training session, but Ginger hated being in a stall at all. She was making the kind of racket only a mule can make. Her loud hee-haws were like an urgent warning of dire emergency. There was a sound of the death rattle about them. I had fallen for Ginger's convincing role as the dying mule before. I had run, heart pounding, to her stall, ready for the worst. Of course, all I found was Ginger's big mule eyes staring at me as if to say, "How kind of you to come visit me." She would then let loose with another hee-haw, knocking me off balance. I think she lured me over just to knock me on my ass. The question is, why did I continue to think she was adorable and seek out her company?

Sam and I were the only humans in a barn full of animals. Most of the Rescue's ten or so goats were there, curious about what was going on with Zeke. Several of the Rescue's sheep were in there with us too. Some hens and a rooster were running around, their random crowing sending a spike up my spine. Then there was Millie the pig. Millie was mad at us for disturbing her day-long nap. She intermittently scolded us. There were also nine horses in the barn. Sam had brought her adorable beagle named Bagel with her to the barn that day and there were always a few cats roaming around.

Sam finished repacking Zeke's hooves with fresh gauze, sealed them with lots of vet tape and screwed on Zeke's last shoe. Galaxy, a huge Clydesdale gelding, had been watching us from a nearby stall. For a mere second, Zeke swung his butt close to Galaxy. I saw the big Clyde stretch out his neck and in a flash of teeth, bite Zeke on the butt. Because horses have near 360-degree peripheral vision, Zeke saw it coming even before he felt it. He answered with a lightning-fast kick backwards, landing it hard on Galaxy's stall door. It sounded like the barn was coming down. Zeke bellowed. Galaxy roared back. Zeke strained at the cross-ties holding him, half bucking to re-position himself for another smack at Galaxy.

All hell broke loose. The goats and the sheep panicked, bleating and baa-ing while bolting for the exits at each end of the barn. Millie chimed in with a sustained squeal at the top of her lungs. The hens and the rooster skittered every which way to get far from the skirmish, squawking and flapping their wings. Nine horses kicked in their stalls and whinnied the high-pitched whinny that stops you in your tracks. Ginger wailed. Bagel barked. Cats scattered. Sam and I yelled at Galaxy and Zeke.

While she would never have said it, Sam seemed to be running on her last nerve. She had been working in the chaos longer that day than I had. I took her quick intake of breath, a wince, and a jerk of the hand to be subtle signs she was done with all this and ready to get out of the barn. It came, however, as no surprise to me that I felt comfortable in this pandemonium. I liked the swirl of activity and the heightened awareness it created. I liked the noise, even though it quite often scared me. I liked the anticipation of what looney, though entertaining, thing could happen next. Nola was teaching me the healing power of stillness and calmness, no doubt. But I could not escape the fact that creative chaos was, and will probably always be, my natural habitat. These sounds and the intense energy in the barn made a comfortable, creative environment that was, to my mind, one of the most intoxicating aspects of the Rescue.

Millie, a 225-pound Pot Belly pig. Millie had her fans, but Millie and I had history.

AVALANCHE

Life Reimagined

In 1956, a big white horse was dumped at the New Holland Horse Auction in Lancaster County, Pennsylvania. His body was scarred and showed signs of years of hard work. No one wanted to buy him. In the end, his owners sold him to the slaughterhouse where horses were killed for their meat.

What happened next led to one of the most famous "second chance" stories in equine history. Mr. Harry de Leyer, late arriving to the auction, asked to see the big white horse already loaded onto the truck headed for the slaughterhouse. When the horse was unloaded and he was able to really see him, Mr. de Leyer took a chance and bought him right there for $80. The horse, later named Snowman by the de Leyer children, went on to become one of the most famous show jumping horses the country has ever known.

In 1958, Snowman won show jumping's triple crown. This abandoned horse, saved from the slaughterhouse, won the American Horse Show Association "Horse of the Year," the Professional Horseman's Association Championship, and was the Champion of Madison Square Garden's Diamond Jubilee. Snowman was later inducted into the Show Jumping Hall of Fame.[3]

3   <u>Snowman: The True Story of a Champion</u>, by Catherine Hapka, Scholastic, Inc. 2017.

Sixty-two years after Snowman's famous rescue, another big white horse was left at that same New Holland Horse Auction. Like Snowman, this horse also showed the scars and exhaustion of grueling work, probably pulling a plow, for owners who did not care about him. Like Snowman, no one bid on him. Like Snowman, he was going to be sold to the slaughterhouse. But people from the Rescue were at the auction that day. They sized up the situation and bought the Percheron gelding so the slaughterhouse could not have him. They named him Avalanche.

Avalanche was in worse shape than Snowman when he left the New Holland Auction. In fact, Avalanche was a mercy buy. Christine thought he was so used-up, the kindest thing might be to give him a quick and painless passing in the calmness of the Rescue. Avalanche, emaciated and banged-up, was an example of how truly wretched some humans could be. It was evil to allow a horse to waste away, to slowly die like that.

When the trailer arrived at the Rescue and he and the other horses saved that day were unloaded, Avalanche went off by himself, shunning the other horses. He stood alone, body slumped, head down. The other horses enthusiastically ate the food they were given soon after settling into the quarantine field. But Avalanche did not eat. He had no interest in food.

He was doing something I had never seen a horse do: he was chewing on the top rail of the wooden fence. I was told he was "cribbing." He was biting the fence while breathing in deeply, like sucking on the fence. When horses do this, endorphins are released that give them a "high." Cribbing can also produce excess saliva that can buffer stomach pain. He was just skin and bones. He had to be in horrible pain. Who could blame him for wanting to escape by getting high? Avalanche was comforting himself as best he could.

Christine liked to give a chance to any horse with a glimmer of hope. Hard decisions about what horses to keep out of the hundreds who needed help were made nearly every day. A lot went into the decision. A horse's condition and chance of success, how much attention and staff time it would take to save a horse, the cost of medical care, how many horses were already in the rehab barn, and adoptability were all factors. But there was room for instinct. Sometimes Christine waited to see how a horse adapted to the Rescue, looking for signs that a rehabilitation program could be successful.

By any measure, it did not look good for Avalanche. His condition was extreme. It would require medicines, food, staff attention, a place in the rehab barn and even then, success was a long shot. And few people wanted to adopt a horse who chewed up their fences by cribbing.

The bigger problem was Avalanche did not seem to want to live. If a horse shrank into the corners or hid behind the run-in shed and would not eat, there was not much anyone could do for him. I felt so sorry for Avalanche, huddling into himself. If his life spark had truly gone out, we had gotten to him too late.

At some point in the next few days, Avalanche decided he wanted to live. He started eating. He moved around the field a bit. He kept cribbing, but he had turned the corner on embracing life. If Avalanche was going to bet on himself, Christine was willing to take a chance on him too.

When his time in quarantine was up, Avalanche was moved into the rehab barn where he could get the special treatment he needed. Starvation cases as extreme as his nearly always had other related health problems that required medication and care. Avalanche did well in rehab. He gained weight and began coming out of himself. He was eventually moved into a field with other horses of varying ages and soundness. This herd was a mix of horses still recovering but not yet sound enough to start training, as well as elderly horses who would never be sound enough to ride. A few of the nurse mare foals who came as tiny babies, now teenagers, were also in this field.

Avalanche adapted well to his new herd. After a while, another white Percheron, who looked very much like him, came to the Rescue and was eventually put into his field. His name was Glacier. Glacier and Avalanche became best buddies. They hung around together and it seemed Avalanche was bringing Glacier along, showing him the ropes. But as Avalanche got stronger, Glacier did not. The pair made a valiant effort, but in the end, Glacier did not make it.

Despite grieving for his friend, Avalanche continued to make progress. He was becoming solid and healthy. Some of the staff began wondering if he was as old as originally thought. His front teeth were a worn-down mess from cribbing. Because the condition of a horse's teeth is a good indication of age, he was pegged as an older horse. He was originally thought to be thirty or older.

However, based on his recovery and on closer inspection, some pegged him at more like eighteen or twenty. Some guessed as low as fifteen.

I had eagerly watched Avalanche since the day he came to the Rescue. The fact that he didn't die that night or the next day was my first surprise. That he adapted to life at the Rescue and outlived Glacier was another surprise. That he was aging backwards was one more surprise. That he was actually getting a bit chunky, shocked the hell out of me. But my biggest surprise was yet to come.

I was walking down the Rescue's driveway one afternoon to the gate of the field creatively called Driveway Field. Only geldings lived in Driveway Field. Most of them were either rideable or in training to be ridden. That meant they were sound and had been approved by the vet for work. Driveway Field was where some of the most badass horses were. There was a definite Alpha horse and an established pecking order in Driveway. Firmly at the top was a huge Belgian-Clydesdale cross named Amble. No one messed with Amble, as he could intimidate any horse in the field. There were also a few younger horses just figuring out their own powers of intimidation, along with a couple of Amble-wannabes who could be aggressive within the herd.

As I got closer, I saw one of our horse trailers stopping at the gate. They were moving a horse from another field into Driveway. It was always interesting to watch how a herd behaved with a new horse. It would have to be a strong horse to make his way in this field of rampant testosterone. I wondered who the horse was. I had to strain a bit to see but, to my horror, they were walking Avalanche down the trailer ramp. They circled him around a bit so he could get his bearings, opened the gate and led him into the Driveway Field.

Avalanche?? That made it a whole different game. What was about to happen had just gone from being interesting to my special boy being thrown to the lions. Images of him huddled up, skinny and alone on his first day flashed across my mind. They were going to kill him in there. In my mind, I could see them going at him one at a time and then, weakened, they would finish him off as a group.

There was already a commotion in the field as the horses sensed something was about to happen. Avalanche trotted around a bit. As I feared, a few horses came at him, teeth bared, ready to fight. Avalanche broke into a gallop.

I had never seen him gallop. Was that their plan, to run him until he was exhausted and then kill my poor baby? Soon the whole field was in chaos. While beating up on Avalanche was still the main attraction, mini rumbles broke out all around the field as some horses used the melee to better their standing in the hierarchy.

I struggled to keep Avalanche in my sight through the mayhem. The horses were still chasing him. He was still running. They kept coming, biting and kicking at him. Amble stayed on the fringe of the skirmishes. Why get involved when the other horses were doing his work for him? Every kick, every bite landing on Avalanche felt like it was landing on me. I couldn't take it. I started yelling to no one in particular that we had to get him out of there. We had to stop this before he collapsed. We had to stop this before I collapsed.

But wait. Something was happening. Avalanche let out a kick on the fly. He turned and started biting back at his tormentors. He nailed more than one. They backed off a bit. Then, he positioned himself just right and started whacking the miscreants with his powerful hind legs. He went after the troublemakers, backing up to them and bucking. He was landing some serious blows. Avalanche was coming on strong. Amazingly, it looked like one of the younger horses actually went over to Avalanche's side and was defending him. This went on for a while, but it was clear the tide had turned. Once they saw he could defend himself, the attacks stopped. Not wanting to take more punishment from the big white newcomer, the herd settled down. Avalanche was not only going to survive, he had established himself as a respected member of the Driveway herd.

I was proud of the way Avalanche bravely defend himself. He seemed like a different horse to the one who came to the Rescue. But, the truth was, he had alwaysbeen this horse. When humans stopped working against him and started working with him, he showed us who he was. I had not gotten much beyond seeing Avalanche as the fragile horse he was the day he came to us. But Rescue staff had sensed he was ready to take on the "good-ol-boys." They knew he was strong enough and that he had the personality to fight for his place in the toughest field at the Rescue.

Even though Avalanche could hang tough with the bad boys, he still needed special care. He had turned into an aggressive eater. Who could blame him after being starved for so long? The problem was, he ate so fast, he often choked. We had to break up his food and add hot water, making it into a mash. We fed him by hand a little bit at a time to slow him down. Providing food is an age-old way of communicating love and feeding him this way, his soft nose in the palm of my hand, increased my connection to him.

All the horses I had partnered with in the Rescue's Partner Program had been adopted, leaving me to find a new one. I was obviously drawn to Avalanche, and I thought partnering with him would be a treat. He had proven he could be a threat to other horses when defending himself, but when we spent time together, he was calm and kind.

When I threw the lead rope over his shoulders, Avalanche stood like he was frozen. He did not need to be tied up no matter how many other horses were in the arena to distract him. I lightly drew my fingernails from the top of his head to his tail. I used an overlapping motion with both hands like I was playing a harp. He was mesmerized, moving his head only when I stopped. My hands absorbed the feel of his soft hair, his muscles and his warmth. If I was serene enough, he would nearly fall asleep. I felt tremendous joy being with this giant white horse doing nothing but quietly stroking him, cleaning his coat, brushing his abundant mane and tail, and picking out his hooves. I was lifted up just seeing how much he liked the attention.

Not long after Avalanche's skirmish in the Driveway Field, Shelby began his retraining as a riding horse. He was willing and caught on quickly. He had smooth, fluid gates. He looked as if he liked to move. He was calm and steady and before long, Shelby asked if I wanted to ride him.

I was excited at the idea of riding Avalanche. I was so wound up, I feared he would sense my heart beating wildly when I entered Driveway Field to get him. I worried I might scare him off or have trouble getting his halter on. I worried for nothing. I didn't have any problem getting him away from the other horses and out of the field. He quietly walked at my side toward the indoor riding arena. Then suddenly, his head shot up and off he bolted! No warning, just off he went. He trotted his beautiful trot right back to the Driveway Field and waited at the gate to get back in.

I had been mistakenly lulled into thinking he was following me. The truth was, I had let my mind wander. While I occasionally lost focus, Avalanche never did. He sensed his moment, and he took it.

To discourage him from doing that again, I was told to put his bridle on right away instead of leading him in a halter up to the arena. That helped, of course, but it was not the real problem. If I did not telegraph to Avalanche exactly what I wanted him to do every minute, he would gladly fill unguided seconds with whatever he wanted to do. No amount of hardware on his head or in his mouth was going to make up for lack of focus or direction from me, in the saddle or on the ground. Riding Avalanche was a mental challenge. I could not zone out for a split second. I had to anticipate the next move and communicate it to him clearly. He made me work. He made me concentrate on what we were doing together. He made me a better rider.

Avalanche flourished at the Rescue. When I went into the Driveway Field to get him, he often came to me, putting his big head down to take the bit and let me put his bridle on. The trust in one another we were developing brought tears to my eyes. When we rode on the trails with other horses, Avalanche was "forward." He always wanted to be in front, leading the way. He was alert, responsive, and he liked to go fast. In time, there was no trace of the tired old plow horse he once had been.

I have heard people say draft horses are dumb as a box of rocks. HA! Avalanche responded so quickly to his training that Shelby took it to another level. The Rescue had a Mounted Archery Team. Avalanche became a reliable and swift ride for the team. This was a big deal. Riders had to rely on their mounted archery horses to smoothly canter in a large circle in an arena around a target guided only by body cues. Riders had to drop the reins and used both hands to aim and shoot an arrow at the bullseye while riding. They couldn't have their mount bolt off or slow down or stray from the circle.

Avalanche had been trained to plow a straight line at a walk in an open field guided by a farmer way behind him. Cantering in a wide circle, responding to leg cues in a noisy indoor arena was a big departure from what he had done most of his life. But Avalanche picked it up quickly. He became a team regular, performing in public at the popular Montgomery County Fair in Maryland for the Rescue's mounted archery exhibitions.

The Montgomery County Fair was not Madison Square Garden and mounted archery was not competitive show jumping. But Avalanche, like Snowman, had gone from work horse to show horse. There was more to him than anyone knew. He just needed us to support him and love him and for us to ask him.

Because Avalanche was so clever, he became a good candidate for a new type of training being developed at the Rescue called "clicker training." It was training based on positive reinforcement. Simply put, when your horse did what you want him to do, you pressed a little device in your hand, making a clicking noise while giving him a small bit of food. I had my doubts this could actually work until Avalanche and I tried it.

It was a bit more complicated with Avalanche because he was still on mash, so instead of bits of grain as a reward, I had to give him sloppy warm grain-globs. I stood by his head in the indoor arena following the directions given by Lauren, the inventive and vivacious staffer who had learned clicker training and brought it to the Rescue. Avalanche was very interested in the mash I had in a container affixed to my waist. He tried to reach across me to get at the food. I waited until he moved his head, even just a little bit, away from the food and quickly use my clicker and give him some mash. It did not take him long to figure out if he did not crowd me and looked away from the food, he would hear a click and get a treat.

I had to be focused and quick so he would make a clear connection between moving his head away and getting a click and a treat. Expanding this principle to other behaviors, Avalanche was soon walking at my side, stopping, backing up, turning left and right, speeding up and slowing down with me, all with no lead rope or anything whatsoever to guide him but the periodic click and food reward. He even trotted around planks of wood on the ground and over a frightening plastic tarp that moved and made a lot of noise.

He was learning to look to me for cues on what he should do. This was done in a noisy arena with five or so other horses and their partners doing their own version of clicker training. The reward-based training was working. This approach reflected the mindset at the Rescue. Coercion is not necessary.

Kindness and patience work.

Avalanche was not just a quick brain. Good food, exercise, regular grooming, being part of a herd, and humans who loved him all worked to make him a handsome horse. He regained the classic good looks of the Percheron. He had a strong, beautifully arched neck. His head was large, but his features were almost delicate. His deep brown eyes were soft. Ironically, given the state he was in when he came, Avalanche exuded strength. It turns out he was also photogenic. His good looks and personality landed him a spot on the very competitive Gentle Giants Draft Horse Rescue Calendar two years in a row.

With all the fun things I was doing with Avalanche, it was easy for me to ignore the increasing pain in my right knee. Denial only works for so long. By the time I dealt with it, I had to have a complete knee replacement. A few weeks before I went in for surgery, Avalanche was adopted. It was jarring to think of him leaving. But I would be away from the Rescue for a few months and I was relieved that someone would be giving him the attention he had come to love. We had to go our separate ways, Avalanche to lush green pastures and trail rides, me to the hospital and rehab. It was like we had switched roles.

Avalanche never became a national phenomenon. His name will never be in lights or on many trophies. But he did beat the heavy odds against him for survival. He showed the whole Rescue and all who met him that if you give a horse a second chance, if the broken things that left him shattered are changed, he will show you what has never before been seen. When you swap cruelty for kindness, a horse may reveal what has gone untapped all along. Snowman and Avalanche flourished in the presence of people who cared for them and loved them. They were changed. Their potential was reassessed, their lives were profoundly re-imagined. They became what no one ever dreamed either of these two horses, so nearly lost, could be.

Avalanche turned a corner and finally started eating.

Avalanche reimagined. Here, he is the breathtaking Mr. July in the Gentle Giants Draft Horse 2018 calendar.

BACK TO THE RESCUE
Holding on to the Dream

As I write this last story, my right leg is propped up on a chair with an ice bag on my knee. I have just had a total knee replacement. This knee is not my first joint to disintegrate. It is my fourth. When I die and they come to harvest my donated organs, they might as well take my joints for scrap metal.

There is a saying that before something good happens, everything has to fall apart. My experience at the Rescue has been different. Everything fell apart "while" something good was happening. Since coming to the Rescue four years ago, I have had two total hip replacements and a knee replacement. That's three joint replacements in four years.

I began falling apart about six months after I started volunteering at the Rescue. I felt a horrible pain in my left hip. I knew this particular pain well, having first felt it about fifteen years earlier in my right hip.

Back then, I had no idea what it was. I spent two years trying to figure it out. It felt like shards of crushed glass packed into my right hip joint, relentlessly stabbing me. I tried everything to get relief: vigorous exercise, rest, occupational therapy, ice packs, heating pads, acupuncture, and every over-the-counter pain reliever, pain patch, and muscle balm on the market. None of it worked. I still found myself clinging to a grocery cart in the COSTCO parking lot crying from the pain.

I started going to a physical therapist. One day, during a physical therapy session, I got stuck on the floor and could not move. My therapist, a bit shook up at seeing me completely immobile on her floor, said we had to change our approach. If we couldn't figure out what was causing the pain, we had to figure out what was not. She said the first thing we should eliminate was arthritis. I was in my early fifties and did not know what arthritis was. But after two years of unsuccessfully searching for an answer, I went to an orthopedic surgeon to at least rule out arthritis and go from there. A series of X-rays showed I had debilitating arthritis. The cushiony cartilage that kept my bones from rubbing on each other had worn out. It was bone grinding on bone that was causing the searing pain in my hip.

The doctor thought I was very young to have that much joint damage, but faced with what the X-rays showed and my pain level, the only option was a full hip replacement. I was stunned. I was incredibly glad to know what was causing the pain that had disrupted my whole life, but how could this be right? Only old people had arthritis. Only the elderly with halitosis and smelling of VapoRub, boiled cabbage, and mothballs got hip replacements. Fifty was supposed to be the new forty, not the new eighty.

Still, there was no question about whether to have the surgery. I wanted whatever was causing this pain gone. I ended up being the youngest patient on the orthopedic ward by about thirty years and the old toothless guy with a half-opened hospital gown supported by an orderly under each arm, kept hitting on me, but I could take it. I would endure almost anything because getting a new right hip meant I would not be sidelined from my own life. The surgery was successful and at age fifty-two, I got my first second chance to live a good life.

Thirteen years after that right hip replacement, I was happily immersed in the delights of the Rescue, getting good at feeding and grooming the horses and all the other everyday chores. I loved holding the horses to keep them calm while the vet and the farrier worked on them. I was taking riding lessons and got good enough to ride a variety of Rescue horses. I was developing special relationships with several horses and I merrily showed visitors around the Rescue. Living my dream, I was enormously happy. Then I felt that stabbing pain in my left hip.

Many people mistakenly think the pelvic bone is the hip bone. Actually, the hip joint is a ball and socket joint in the butt. I found it particularly cruel that now, when literally so much was riding on my rear end, the crippling pain I had known so well thirteen years ago was back, only this time in my left hip. I tried to ignore it, denying the pain for many months. I raged against my bad luck for a few more months, then finally, I went to the doctor. He confirmed what I already knew. I would have to have my left hip replaced.

The hip replacement surgery went well except for one thing. I didn't notice it until I was home from the hospital. When I took the first step on my own, without the walker, it became obvious one leg was longer than the other. It must have been part of the post-op swelling or something. When, after five days, there was still a noticeable difference in the length of my legs, I called my doctor's assistant.

She said it was completely normal for me to feel like one leg was longer than the other. She said there might be a small discrepancy in the lengths, but that a lot of it was just getting used to the new hip joint.

I wasn't buying it. There was no way I was imagining this. I ordered shoe inserts from Amazon. I stacked all of them in one shoe to make up for that leg being shorter. But I had not gotten enough. I looked around the house for what else I could put in my shoe, which was when I spied the cleaning sponge on the kitchen sink. It was a bright yellow sponge on one side and had a dark gritty substance on the other. I pulled a clean one from the cabinet and put it in my shoe, wrapper and all. That did it. My shoe was tightly packed and it squeaked, but I no longer wobbled when I walked.

Even so, something wasn't right. After getting a whole new hip made of the latest high-performance plastics and titanium, I was relying on a kitchen sponge bought in bulk from Costco to make the whole thing work. I called my doctor again to let him know I had measured my leg length discrepancy at 1.5 inches. That got his attention. He made an appointment for me with a specialist at the rehabilitation center in the hospital where I had my surgery. I wish I had a video of the specialist's face when I took my shoe off and pulled out two cork inserts, two plastic insoles, a gel cushion and, dramatically, my bright yellow kitchen sponge.

After several tries, the specialist was able to construct a custom orthotic for my shoes that came close to evening up my legs. I was not thrilled about this. But the contraption fit into my riding and muck boots and got me back to the Rescue.

Fast forward five months. I started feeling twinges in my right hip again, the one I had replaced thirteen years ago. I knew those preliminary twinges well—I was a freaking expert on those twinges. Not again! This was so unfair. I had only been back at the Rescue for a couple of months since my last surgery. I was just getting back into the routine and making up for lost time. Was my sacrifice of two hips not enough to satisfy the Joint Gods? Now they wanted a third?

As improbable as this seemed, I knew what the twinges meant. My butt never lied. Again, after many months of denial, followed by more months of being ticked off, I went to the doctor. It was incomprehensible to me that I had worn out the plastic ball and socket replacement joint in my right hip. What on earth was I doing to grind down a plastic and titanium joint? My husband has run twelve marathons. He started when he was fifty. Is he grinding the crap out of his joints? No, he is not! What's up with me?

Recovery from the "update" of the replacement hip, known as a revision, was far worse than the recovery from the original hip replacement. Because my bones had grown around the first artificial joint, as they were supposed, we had to be very careful to ensure my bones were not damaged during surgery or in rehab. I had to keep 100% of my weight off my hip for basically six weeks. That would be followed by eight weeks of fiendish physical therapy to rebuild everything that had atrophied during a month and a half stuck in bed.

The doctor was serious about not putting any weight on my hip. We had to hire a haulage company to move me, in my wheelchair, from the hospital to the second floor of our house where I would reside for the next six weeks. A large windowless commercial van came to get me at the hospital. It had what looked like railroad tracks laid on the van floor. To keep me from rolling around in the van, they used massive steel clips to secure me and my wheelchair to the rails.

Our house sat on a hill. There were a lot of steps. There was a set of steps off the sidewalk just to get to the five front porch steps. Inside the house there were three more sets of stairs and two landings to negotiate. I could not stay on the first floor because there was no bathroom. The two beefy haulage company guys strained to get me and my chair up all the stairs. They were steep with banisters and two big newel posts to maneuver around. The stairs zigzagged so the guys had to reposition me at each landing. The staircase was an architectural delight, one of my favorite things about the house. But that day, I was afraid it might kill these two nice guys just trying to do their job without dumping me out of the wheelchair onto my stitched-up butt. While the men stopped to rest on the second landing, contemplating how they were going to position me to get up the last set of stairs, I said goodbye to the first floor of the house for the foreseeable future.

A month and a half later, a bit shriveled up, I started physical therapy. During the intake interview, I was asked what my recovery goal was, what I was hoping to be able to do when I regained my strength. I said I wanted to get back to the Rescue and I wanted to ride again. I showed my therapist pictures of the Rescue and my favorite horses. My goal of getting back to the Rescue became her goal as well.

My intense desire to return helped me endure months of brutal physical therapy. "Back to the Rescue" became the mantra I repeated through clenched teeth laying on a hard table while my skinny physical therapist jammed her sharp elbows deep into my sore muscles.

It would take me three months to return to the Rescue after this surgery. I did have some "poor me" moments, but mostly I was enormously grateful there was a reasonable way to deal with my failing joints that spared me from life in a wheelchair. Thanks to all the painful physical therapy, I did get back to the Rescue and eventually, I could ride again. I had been given a third second chance to live a good life.

There was a silver lining to this miserable ordeal. While he was revising my right hip, the doctor fixed my uneven legs. I am shorter now, but I don't tilt.

Although I had a few physical challenges, I was anxious not to be defined by them. I did not want to be "poor Sarah, always in the hospital." But I knew the pain and the multiple surgeries had changed me. I remember being asked by my doctor to fill out a form prior to my knee surgery. One section asked me to describe what I thought defined me as a person. There was a time I would have answered "strength." But this time, I put "kindness."

Over my four-decade career, I orchestrated power plays and strategic maneuvers. I had thrown the occasional sharp elbow and succeeded in an intensely competitive environment fueled by "experts" and pundits who loved to publicly announce who was "in" and who was "out," who was "up" and who was "down." People's careers rose and fell on those stupid rankings. It was a world of winners and losers where kindness was considered a weakness. Most of my closest colleagues and I never bought into that way of thinking. It was destructive and never got the best results. But it was a popular mindset and fighting against it was exhausting.

At the outset of this book, I said I was not looking for the Rescue, that I didn't even know it existed. I would not have been able to tell you what I was looking for. But I knew it when I found it, or when it found me. The Rescue was a place where kindness replaced competition. It was a way of life, modeled every day.

At the Rescue, like nowhere else I have ever been, kindness was power. A devastated horse like Tonka could be reclaimed. A discarded plow horse like Avalanche became a dependable trail horse. Kindness turned a mistreated horse in a nightmare situation like Atticus into a graceful dressage mount capturing many hearts. It allowed a lame mare destined for slaughter like Dawn to give birth to an adorable foal like Apollo and six little orphaned nurse mare foals from Kentucky to take over the Rescue, enchanting us all. Relentless kindness, day after day, week after week, turned a fearful mare like Nola into a love bug. Kindness made good things happen.

The Rescue could not function without kindness, and neither could I. My joints could come and go, my strength could wax and wane, but the need to express myself through kindness had settled on me and was now a constant.

I am not saying the Rescue was a fairytale place where no one ever got mad and people always got along. We are human. Humans fight and act badly, and we at the Rescue were no exception. But never with the animals. The horses got our best.

As mentioned before, Christine likes to say our horses had just fallen on hard times. She said they should not be defined by that. They have not always been the horse we saw at the Rescue and they will not always be that horse. The Rescue will change them. Hard times can come to anyone and to any horse. Given half a chance, our horses would recover and go on to live the second act of their lives, whatever that may be.

I sympathize. I am not a victim of my arthritic joints. In fact, in some respects, I should be grateful for them. Without the medically necessary forced incarcerations, I might not have stopped moving long enough to reflect on my experiences at the Rescue. The horses, ever on my mind, became my constant companions during my isolation. I thought about them, scrolling through thousands of pictures of them on my cell phone, and soon, I began writing about them. They took me out of myself while my own body, like the horses at the Rescue, healed.

The Rescue has offered me a chance to embrace a dream. Having three major surgeries in four years has offered me good reasons to give up on that dream. But I didn't. I don't know if this is the end. More joints may disintegrate. My other knee will probably give out and my shoulders could go. But I am okay with that. I'll adapt. I recently read something attributed to author Marianne Williamson: "Ego says, 'Once everything falls into place, I will feel peace.' Spirit says, 'Find your peace, and everything will fall into place.'" Maybe when it looked to me like things were falling apart, they were actually falling into place.

Now, the ice pack on my knee has melted and is wobbling around. It won't be long before my knee is no longer the size of a football and I will not need to ice it every day. The long, curvy, kind of ugly incision will heal and there will be only a slight scar left to memorialize the operation. My love-hate relationship with my physical therapist will evolve into only gratitude. I will get strong again. And I will go, patched up and happy, back to the Rescue.

Photo by Adria Strausbaugh

The End

ACKNOWLEDGEMENTS

First, I want to thank Judy Navarro whose encouragement and cheerful support motivated me to write about my adventures at the Rescue. Judy is herself an avid reader and writer who worked many years in the publishing business. Her objective evaluation meant a great deal to me. But her good humor and reassurance that people would be interested in what happened to the horses and the people at the Rescue made me keep going.

I also want to thank my good friend, Trina Ramsey, networker extraordinaire, for her enthusiasm about the book and for her no-nonsense approach to making good things happen. At dinner together one evening, I asked her if there was anyone she had worked with when she wrote and published her book, *Just Do You! A Declaration of Independence from Guilt, Obligation, and Shame*. Before we ordered dessert, she had a meeting set up for me with her editor.

Kim Brown, Executive Editor of Minerva Rising Press, and I met because neither of us could say no to Trina. But we quickly developed a rapport of our own that turned into a marvelous working relationship. Kim has been invaluable as an editor and teacher. She turned problems I thought were insurmountable into small irritants quickly dispatched. But for her guidance and talent, my stories might have remained in a large three-ring binder on my bookshelf with papers sticking out, like an abandoned scrapbook project.

I am grateful to my longtime friends Kathy Gille and Paula Short for the gift of letting me see the Rescue through their eyes on an eventful trip we shared to the Rescue. And thanks to Kathy for listening to me moan about writer's block and for her wise tips on dealing with it. And thanks to Allison Remsen who does not know a horse from a hyena, but never waivers in her support for whatever project I am doing.

I thank another longtime friend, Katherine Wittneben. We have had many escapades together over a lot of years and I appreciate her support and her belief in me and in this book.

Thanks also to Lauren Coletta for helping me cope with computers, clouds, chromes and dropboxes, which left on my own, could make me cry.

I am also grateful to Rosemary Freeman, Sue Smock, and Marda Robillard, my friends for over forty years, for their feedback on early chapters. And thanks to Christopher and Carmel Mansour for tracking my progress and their unwavering enthusiasm and humor.

 My twist on the old adage "it takes a village" is "it takes a farm." My energy and insight for writing the book came from the extraordinary animals and people I met at the Rescue. Special thanks to Christine Hajek, President and Founder of the Gentle Giants Draft Horse Rescue, for all her help with this book. Her expertise at finding photos and providing technical information was invaluable. But most important, I thank her for having the vision and drive to establish the Rescue and share it with all of us. Thousands of people here and around the world are inspired by what she started.

Big thanks to Christina Wheeler Rizzutto, who took me on as a riding student after my incident with Twinkie. I felt I was doing well to be riding with a prosthetic hip until I found out a horse once reared up, fell backwards on top of Christina, breaking her back, and she is still riding. I also appreciate her for providing much needed technical information.

I want to express my profound gratitude to the staff and volunteers who make it a joy to come to the Rescue. They are fierce and mighty, strong and intrepid, gentle and patient. They inspired me with grace and humor, to suck it up and keep on moving.

I am grateful to Jessica Hunter Hinsvark for her cover photo of Thunder, our Red Shire. Through her photographer's eye and her horse lovers' heart, she captured his power, his playfulness and the secret something that makes a horse like Thunder unforgettable. I am honored to have him galloping across the book cover, leading the way to the Rescue.

A hearty thank you to the fantastic volunteer photographers who generously shared their work to bring extra life to the stories and characters in the book. And to everyone who participated in the email chain figuring out who took which photos.

Thanks to the many horses at the Rescue who make my dream come true. They continue to touch my heart and make me a better person.

And thank you to my husband, Alan Kadrofske, who has been with me on this adventure since we first drove to the Rescue that fateful day four years ago. His editorial comments about this book have been right on the nose. But he is absolutely wrong when he insists my riding boots stink up the car. I smell only a rich, sweet aroma that immediately takes me to a place I love.

ABOUT THE AUTHOR

Sarah Dufendach was born and educated near Detroit, Michigan, but worked most of her professional life in Washington D.C. She was Chief of Staff for many years to Rep. David Bonior, the Democratic Whip of the U.S. House of Representatives. She served as the Chief Operating Officer for the Vietnam Veterans of America Foundation, Vice President for Government Relations at Common Cause, and V.P. for Federal Relations at the University of Maryland University College, (UMUC).

Finding her inner cowgirl, Sarah traded her high heels and business suits for a pair of muck boots and some riding pants, and her big office for a horse barn. She lives in Northern Virginia with her husband Alan Kadrofske and their adored Keeshond dog named Harry Pawter.

www.ingramcontent.com/pod-product-compliance
Lightning Source LLC
Chambersburg PA
CBHW061236270326
41930CB00021B/3480